THE ORIGIN OF
CIVILIZED SOCIETIES

THE ORIGIN
OF CIVILIZED
SOCIETIES

RUSHTON
COULBORN

PRINCETON, NEW JERSEY
PRINCETON UNIVERSITY PRESS
1959

Publication of this book
has been aided by the Ford Foundation program
to support publication,
through university presses, of works in the
humanities and social sciences

✧

Printed in the United States of America
by Princeton University Press, Princeton, N.J.

To

Alfred Louis Kroeber

PREFACE

EVERY book which deals with major events in the career of man is a product of its age. It must discuss its subject from a point of view which contemporary events have formed. The subject itself may be dictated, whether or not the author is conscious of dictation, by the concern of his society with some great current issue.

The subject of this book is quite remote from world politics. There is not a word in it on such a matter. The subject nevertheless falls into place among those which current relations between the world's peoples have brought into debate. When the Western Society, which is to say, the peoples of the European cultural descent, obviously led the world, civilization seemed to be a condition or a quality in which that society excelled. But the faltering of Western leadership and especially the breakdown of the Western imperialist dispensation have thrown doubt upon the quality of Western civilization, and brought into debate the substance and the concept of civilization itself.

No part of the debate has been more difficult than that concerning origins. I first set out to write about it in 1944, but after some struggle put the subject aside for lack of sufficient secure data. In the succeeding decade, however, a number of new discoveries and a few important new syntheses were made by specialist scholars, particularly about the civilized societies of the New World. Brought together, these have made possible a coherent treatment of the origin of civilized societies. It remains, inevitably, a treatment in which some quite important questions are merely raised and discussed, and are then left unresolved.

Two questions of the first importance are answered decisively. One is whether there is a distinction between civilized and primitive societies and the other whether civilized societies were of single or multiple origin. The answer to the first question is that there is a distinction, but that it cannot be stated correctly in any short theoretical formula, and to the second that civilized societies were of multiple origin. Both questions are answered together with a historical account of the emergence of the seven "primary" civilized societies out of a foregoing regime of primitive societies, the novelties being shown comparatively among the seven.

These decisions and others in the book must in the course of time come to have a bearing upon the large practical issues of recent times which ultimately brought attention to the matters in question—that is to say, the decisions must do so if there proves to be any sound substance in them. Any attempt here to forecast the results of their influence would, however, be presumptuous and might well prove nugatory.

There is one more aspect of the book which deserves attention here, a technical aspect, but not, certainly, one which only concerns scholars. The book is written in the form of a comparison. As between civilized societies comparison is of paramount importance. There have been in history only fourteen fully distinct civilized societies (the number may vary a little according to what is taken to be full distinction). Among such small numbers there is little use for general classifications, such as readily arise among physical and biological phenomena and, less readily, among minor social phenomena. A few civilized societies, or indeed all civilized societies, may be classed together on the ground of their likenesses, but their inevitable unlikenesses may never, or scarcely ever, be ignored, as may the unlikenesses of phenomena which are usefully classified. Thus, comparison is the ultimate theoretical operation which is useful for understanding civilizations and civilized societies; which is to say that it is the best way of understanding history, for what is conventionally called history is the history of civilized societies from the time when they began to leave written evidence of themselves.

That does not mean, of course, that all historical study is, or should be, comparison. Fact-finding is the fundamental operation in historical study, and narrative description the most usual form for presenting its results. Comparison may indeed serve secondarily as a directive in fact-finding, for it may indicate where in narrative sequences new fact is most needed and should therefore be sought. Thus, comparison is the most obvious and effective complement to fact-finding and narrative; it is a wholly theoretical operation, whereas fact-finding is essentially practical and narrative is for the most part preliminary theory. In reality, this relationship always existed, but historians have tended to stop short with narrative and, until recently, to be extremely casual, not to say careless and unscientific, in the occasional use of comparison they made. I very much hope that this book, although it is confined to the beginning of history—to prehistory indeed if conventional distinctions are to be observed—will encourage historians to undertake serious comparative works and other interested persons to demand comparative works from historians.

I am very grateful to those friends who have been good enough to read and criticize the manuscript of the book. Professor A. L. Kroeber and Professor Crane Brinton both read a full draft of the book. These first readings are extremely important to me, for I suffer from a constitutional difficulty in reducing arguments to readable proportions. Mr. Kroeber and Mr. Brinton made almost identical criticisms of the draft, and I was persuaded and shown at once what I ought to do with it. Professor Charles Le Guin of the University of Idaho helped me to simplify Chapter i. My colleague Professor Melvin Watson of Morehouse College and Professor William Bradley of the Hartford Seminary Foundation read the manuscript and gave me their valuable opinions and suggestions upon what appears about religion in the book. I have discussed parts of the material with colleagues and students on ordinary academic occasions at Atlanta University, and have profited largely from doing so. Mr. Benjamin F. Houston, as editor for the Princeton University Press, gave valuable counsel about the whole manuscript and helped me in particular to improve its form.

Without the generous financial support of several foundations the book could not have been written, or it would still be in the early stages of composition. The Rockefeller Foundation gave me a fellowship during a sabbatical year, 1956-1957, in which I covered the largest special task included in the book, the treatment of religion. In other years I have had three grants-in-aid from the Penrose Fund of the American Philosophical Society, one each from the Social Science Research Council and the American Council of Learned Societies, and grants from the Atlanta University Research Fund. I have thus been enabled to travel freely in order to collect material for the book.

I am also much indebted to Columbia University for free use of its broad library resources. Most of the collection of material and some of the writing of the book have been done at Columbia.

Finally, I want to thank the ladies who, with little or no material reward, have typed the manuscript, bearing heroically with the intrinsic difficulties of the subject matter and with the idiosyncrasies of my temperament, my mode of composition, and my penmanship.

R. C.

Atlanta University
October 1958

CONTENTS

THE ORIGIN OF
CIVILIZED SOCIETIES

CIVILIZED MAN AND

HIS HISTORY

CIVILIZED SOCIETIES have been in existence for about six or six and a half millennia. It cannot be doubted that they are the greatest social achievement humanity has yet made. According to the criteria of differences used in this study, there have been fourteen distinct civilized societies, or a few more if certain minor formations are counted.[1] Of the fourteen, four exist today fully recognizable, and remnants of a few others in recognizable, or unrecognizable, shapes.

The term "civilized" is reserved here for the large societies to be identified forthwith, and the term "civilization" for their high culture considered abstractly.

The earliest civilized societies were the Egyptian and Mesopotamian societies, which arose in the valleys respectively of the Nile and of the Tigris and Euphrates, probably in the fifth millennium B.C. It is not possible to decide whether one was earlier than the other; nor, for most purposes, would it be particularly useful to do so. The Indian Society arose first in the valley of the Indus where that river passes through

[1] Robert Heine-Geldern has recently argued that all civilization originated in the Near East of the Old World and was thereafter diffused elsewhere. This egregious error is discussed below; see pp. 27ff.

Sind and the Punjab and possibly also in the valley of a now dry sister river of the Indus, usually called the Great Mihran by those who think it existed.[2] Whether the Indian Society originated earlier, later, or about the same time as the Egyptian and Mesopotamian societies is not known, but possibly a few centuries later.

The Cretan Society arose in the island of Crete and subsequently extended into the Cyclades, the Peloponnese, and perhaps elsewhere. It originated about 3000 B.C. or somewhat earlier.[3] The Chinese Society arose in the Yellow River Valley and on the river's tributaries in north China where the river passes between Shensi and Shansi and through Honan. Its time of origin is not clear, but is most likely to have been in the first half of the third millennium B.C.

In the New World two other societies arose. The Middle American Society arose somewhere within a broad territory beginning in the north with the Mexican states of Vera Cruz, Guanajuato, and Michoacan, and covering the rest of Mexico southward and eastward, British Honduras, Guatemala, Honduras, and some of El Salvador. It is becoming clear that the society was much scattered within this territory from an early time in its existence.

The Andean Society arose in all likelihood on three or

2 Cf. Sir John Marshall, *Mohenjo-Daro and the Indus Civilization* (London, 1931), I, 5-6. V. G. Childe (*New Light on the Most Ancient East*, new ed., London, 1952, p. 172) writes in brackets after "Gt. Mihran" "Sarasvati," hoping thus, I suppose, to solve an old puzzle.

3 The date suggested is chosen in the light of R. W. Hutchinson's chronology ("Minoan Chronology Reviewed," *Antiquity*, XXVIII [1954], 155-164), but with some misgiving. Hutchinson says, "2900? [B.C.] Early Neolithic begins in Knosos" (p. 164). The figure he chooses is based partly on cross-datings with Egypt, the Egyptian dates being secured on Carbon-14 runs. I do not think enough carbon dates for effective cross-correlation have yet been found for the Near East; I am inclined to think that those which have been found give general indications which are rather too low; and no carbon dates can (by the present scientific method) give dates sufficient to warrant preferring as little as a century's variation from a round figure such as 3000.

more rivers which cross the northern part of the Peruvian coastal desert, the rivers Chicama, Moche, and Virú and perhaps others. Eventually the society extended to the valleys of some thirty-five odd rivers which cross the desert farther south, and also moved up and well over the Andes. These two societies originated during the second millennium B.C., the Middle American Society towards the beginning of the second millennium, and the Andean Society towards the end of it.

Following Toynbee and Alfred Weber, I call these seven societies the primary civilized societies since they were, each within its general region, the earliest civilized societies. This book is a study of how the seven primary civilized societies arose; it is a study, that is to say, of how civilization began. The societies arose in very special circumstances, of which the chief was change of climate in certain regions at the end of the last Pleistocene Ice Age. The regions are today desert or steppe, and it was their conversion to that dry condition which drove some of their human inhabitants to make a long series of cultural and social changes, to migrate in various directions and on a number of occasions, and eventually to form civilized societies.

Chapter 2 is a survey of the changes of climate and of the rise and spread of mesolithic culture and of the early agri-cultures which preceded the formation of the primary civilized societies. Chapters 3 and 4 contain examinations of the physi-ography of the seven sites and of the archaeological and other data which throw light on how settlement in the sites came about. A highly important consideration about the origin of the societies is that the seven sites were all difficult for human inhabitation and that they had no regular human inhabitants until the founders of the seven societies, or their immediate forbears, migrated into them and established themselves there.

I hold that in the course of migration and settlement in the

5

sites of the seven societies new religions were formed. The tenuous and difficult evidence for that opinion is examined in Chapter 5, and there is a preliminary discussion in this introductory chapter of the ground for supposing that religions were built up at the origin of the societies. This chapter is, in fact, a more ample preparation for the main substance of the book than introductory chapters usually are. The reason for this is that it is necessary both to introduce the circumstances in which the primary civilized societies originated and to show what civilized societies are. The latter is the chief special task which has to be undertaken here, but neither of these subjects is at all fully known; nor is there any substantial agreement among scholars upon what is known about them. To elucidate them effectively here it is necessary to anticipate the findings of later chapters occasionally, but no novel assumptions are made which are not later justified, so far as the evidence allows.

The seven primary civilized societies have had varied histories. Two still exist today, but the other five have been succeeded by essentially new societies. The two which still exist are the Indian and Chinese societies. Both have extended vastly beyond their original sites, which were river valleys, and have come into contact with each other on a wide front. Like all other civilized societies, they fell into decline after rising to a certain high level of efflorescence, and then revived and moved again on to a high level and again thereafter into decline, and so on. Probably both the Indian and Chinese societies have been through three successive "cycles" of rise, efflorescence, and fall, but the Chinese Society may only have been through two; what happened in its earliest centuries remains obscure. The term "cycle" is used in this study without implication of mechanism or of mathematical system, but simply as a common-sense word for the up and down movements characteristic of the historical development of civilized societies.

The three westerly primary societies of the Old World gave place eventually to new societies although both the Egyptian and Mesopotamian societies passed through two cycles, the Egyptian through a third, vestigial one, and the Mesopotamian virtually through a third, in which, however, the civilization was so much modified that I change the name in that cycle to Iranian. Among the westerly Old World societies, in fact, the succession of cycles has been vastly complicated by a number of influences, the most powerful of which has been contact of expanding societies with others, leading to intrusion and interpenetration, often with violence, and often over great areas of territory. One consequence of this has been combination and reconstitution of culture as between two or more societies and emergence of new civilizations which cannot be called, with any show of reason, by the name of one of those from which they were derived. So, the three primary societies of the region eventually disappeared, being accompanied in their later cycles and then succeeded, at various times between the second millennium B.C. and the present day, by the Hebrew, Graeco-Roman, Iranian, Byzantine, Western (or European), Islamic, and Russian societies.

This individuation will be disputed by some scholars, but it is one which does little violence to the facts, while accounting well for all important events. Civilization differs in all cases to some extent between cycles, whether the cycles are said to be successive cycles in the history of the same society, or whether they are said to belong to different, but related— more or less successive—societies. Where the difference is less, the same name is used for the society in the two successive cycles in question; where the difference is greater, a new name is used for the society in the later cycle, and in each case of greater difference the new society derived its civilization from more than the one predecessor, even if the one predecessor contributed most. I find this a tolerably satisfactory way of describing, roughly and generally, how civilization has changed in the course of the history of the westerly societies of the Old World. I find too that the distinctions so made between societies are all distinctions which have long had currency among historians—but not, of course, that all distinctions historians have been in the habit of using are thus brought into use here.

The succession among the westerly societies of the Old World is not a regular one. A certain tendency toward regularity of succession is certainly inherent in the development of all civilized societies, but in the region now in question the jostling of different societies has not only brought about mixing and reconstitution of culture; it has also altered, warped, and in some sequences of events very largely overcome the tendency toward regularity of cyclical succession. Thus, there are not, in this region, clear-cut eras of secondary and tertiary cycles or societies to succeed to the era of the primary societies. Again, the same factor of forceful contact between societies is mainly responsible for interruption of the rise and fall process within some cycles in various societies' history, and for irregularities of other kinds which need not be introduced here. But, in spite of all the irregularities and odd formations in the history of this great civilized region, the tendency to regular succession of cycles and to succession within cycles of similar phases, marked by characteristic institutions, arts and ideas, has always been present, is able to reassert itself when opportunity offers, and can usually be discerned as one of the chief influences upon events even in notably distorted successions.

The societies of the New World have had, until the present time, careers which are simplicity itself by comparison with the careers of the societies of the westerly end of the Old

8

World, simple even by comparison with the careers of the Indian and Chinese societies. The Andean and Middle American societies did not outlive their primary cycles. They were in contact with each other, but non-contiguously, so that there was no physical impingement of either upon the other. Both went through rise and efflorescence and then entered upon decline, but before signs of revival appeared, the Western intrusion brought the two societies to an end. It should be observed, however, that this does not mean that there can be no reminiscence of them in future social formations. Such reminiscences have arisen in the Old World, and the violent contact of the Western society with the societies in the New World may have special consequences yet to come.

Every primary civilized society was formed by the amalgamation, in a special kind of environment, of a large number of primitive societies; the term "conglomeration" will be applied here to the formative process. There have been many kinds of primitive societies in the human career. Anthropologists are accustomed to use such terms as "folk" or "non-literate" to denote all of them together, but there will be little occasion in this study for those usages. The primitive societies involved in the origin of civilized societies were among the most advanced societies of their times. They were of tens, hundreds, perhaps sometimes of thousands of persons, organized, at least when settled, on some kind of kinship basis. They were able to live in sedentary villages fixed as to place for a period of years, but all those involved in the origin of civilized societies were, or had recently been, migrants from other places to the sites in which the civilized societies arose. All, or almost all, of them had grain agriculture.

All of them were very largely dependent upon grain agriculture for their subsistence, but the grains they raised varied from region to region, chiefly wheat and barley in the westerly region of the Old World and in India, one or more millets and kaoliang, possibly barley, even possibly rice, in China, maize in the New World. They all raised other vegetables also, but their dependence on these varied widely from case to case. In fact, except for the large dependence on grain raising, all their common activities varied much from group to group. Thus, none of them could maintain their villages—those they occupied before migration to the sites of the future civilized societies—in the same place indefinitely, for after some years they would have exhausted the soil by repeated cropping. How soon a village had to move must have varied greatly, however, chiefly with the quality of the soil, but also to some extent with varying methods of cultivation. Most villages increased rather rapidly in population, but the rate of increase probably varied a good deal as between different regions. Parts of the increased population could and certainly did hive off from time to time, but the consequent increase in a whole district required general expansion, and must have led to longer and longer and more and more dangerous migrations. Probably some villagers had to move as often as every three years, the majority at all sorts of intervals up to a generation and more.

All the villagers had pottery, but it varied a great deal in quality; in most cases it was good. They all made cloth by spinning and weaving, or by variations of those practices. Certainly, they did not all have domesticated animals: in the New World such animals were very few, or entirely lacking; in the Old World, they varied from region to region, but were numerous in the westerly region. All the villagers hunted, and continued to hunt after the civilized societies emerged, but their reliance upon game for food must have varied a good deal. Their modes of housing themselves varied, but that perhaps does not matter very much for present purposes.

All the primitive societies had beliefs about the physical

world in which they lived, beliefs which required the existence of controlling powers, not easily discernible to man, but actively interested in man's doings, and prepared to interfere if man did things they did not like. Undoubtedly, all the societies were much concerned with the attitude of the controlling powers toward the growth of the plants cultivated.

It is not known for certain that grain agriculture was a necessary basis for the formation of a civilized society, but it looks, on the evidence, as if this were so. On the Andean coastal plain, near the mouths of the rivers in whose valleys the civilized society subsequently arose—but very probably not in the valleys themselves—a series of very simple societies, having agriculture but not grain agriculture, established themselves about 2500 B.C. They probably made some sort of use of the rivers, but they continued to live in their simple way for a thousand years without change and without producing any sign—visible to archaeologists—of the beginnings of civilized life. The environment for civilization was at hand, but the peoples had not the cultural basis on which to begin to create a civilization: this is how the situation appears, but the assumption that it was so remains an informed assumption, nothing more. Guesses that there were "marsh Arabs" in southern Mesopotamia, or "fen-dwellers" on the lower Yellow River in China, before the grain cultivators came and settled there are quite insubstantial. Mesolithics and palaeolithics lived indeed in the Kom Ombo Plain, contiguous to the Upper Nile in Nubia, for millennia, and palaeolithics lived near the Indus at Rohri and Sukkur in northern Sind. It seems reasonable to think that palaeolithics and mesolithics, and (if any) fen-dwellers and marsh Arabs, lacked the cultural basis from which to begin the creation of a civilized society, however alluring or compulsive the environment in which they found themselves.

It deserves mention, even though it is abundantly obvious,

11

that a culture having grain agriculture together with an assortment of other useful practices did not of itself by some inherent determinism move on to civilization. Vast numbers of primitive societies with such cultures survived for thousands of years with little change; some survive even now. These things have to be borne in mind because the majority of current books on the subject still describe civilization as a bundle of culture traits, many of them throwing in agriculture without adequate distinction from the rest. In this book agriculture will be treated (in Chapter 2) separately as, to the best of our understanding, the key achievement of man preliminary to civilization, while civilization itself will not be considered as a sum of culture traits.

Another caution, but a less obvious one: civilized societies arose within very special physical environments, but that does not mean that every time grain-cultivating primitives arrived in such an environment a civilized society resulted. We have a relatively good knowledge of the early settlements in the Nile valley; perhaps our knowledge covers something about all of them. The first three types of settlers, all grain-raisers, showed no signs of creating a civilized society even though they lived in their new habitat for some centuries. Of course, they may have entered on a course toward civilization; there is, it may be supposed, more likelihood that they did so than that the earliest, non-grain-raising settlers on the Andean coast did so: the difficulty may merely be that there are no signs of it which an archaeologist can detect.

Again, there are grain-raisers and grain-raisers, and perhaps some grain-raisers could not rise to the initiation of civilization. If they could not, then perhaps their methods of cultivation were not good enough, or perhaps some other trait we have not perceived was needed as well as grain-cultivation. Or, yet again, perhaps there were crucial differences between the various sites, even perhaps between the various river valley sites, in which civilized societies arose, such that for some sites greater preliminary attainments on the part of the settlers were required than for other sites. Here we reach the sphere of the unknown.

Ignorance, then, is freely admitted. But certain suggestions may be made as a start toward dispelling it. One is that the primitives who left their old habitats and migrated to the special kinds of place in which civilized societies arose probably did so because they were in some danger; their survival may have been threatened, and they may have migrated in a state of great agitation. I think it may be taken for granted at least that there were strong reasons for the migrations and that the reasons were not in themselves pleasant; the migrants were not, for example, people getting along fairly well in their old habitat who developed an optimistic conviction that life would be even better in some other place. As we have already seen, the migrations were undertaken at a time of desiccation so that the likelihood of threats to their survival is a large one.

A second suggestion is that the migration from the old habitat to the new is unlikely to have been easy. It is unlikely to have allayed fears, if any, with which the migrants set out. There may well have been casualties on the way; there almost certainly were on some of the migrations. Some whole groups of migrants may have got lost in deserts and died en route, but this is only of significance for the origin of civilized societies if it was known to other groups who got through with some success to the new habitat; it may have been known to them.

A third suggestion is that on migration a social organization different from that of a settled society, even of a settled society which expects to migrate from time to time, is needed. This may have been of little consequence in the case of very short migrations—and some of the migrations were short—

but it can have been of large consequence in cases where they were not short. The old bonds of primitive societies may have weakened somewhat, and possibly there were leaders on the migrations who acquired more authority than the elders of a more or less sedentary clan or tribe.[4]

A fourth suggestion is that the new habitats were in no case easy to settle in; this follows from the assumption, already made, that simpler peoples could not make much of them and in known cases probably settled on the outer edge of the site and not right in it. This suggestion is one founded on a fair amount of evidence. The most important evidence is of adaptation to the conditions of water supply. Such matters will be subject to special study in Chapters 3 and 4. Here it need only be added that conditions in the new habitat, however much they varied from case to case, are unlikely to have eased the fears and anxieties we have supposed the migrants to have experienced before and during their migrations—even if the conditions may soon have become such as to set up hopes alongside the fears, or effectively to nourish hopes which already existed. Nor, if any special discipline was developed on migration, were conditions in the new habitat such as to encourage its loosening.

Finally, out of these various suggestions about fears, hopes, and discipline a thesis may be proposed to the effect that new religious developments probably arose in the minds of the migrants before they left their old homes, while they were migrating, and after their resettlement. It is possible to find support for this thesis in surviving myths and from archaeological sources. That evidence will be thoroughly explored, chiefly in Chapter 5. Analogies, too, are powerful enforce-

---

[4] So we might suppose if we compare the early migrations in question with those undertaken in later history in the "heroic ages" which preceded in some regions the revival of civilized societies after declines; cf. H. M. Chadwick, *The Heroic Age* (Cambridge, Eng., 1912); Rushton Coulborn, ed., *Feudalism in History* (Princeton, 1956), Part III, *passim.*

ments of the thesis, and these may be briefly outlined at once.

The most telling analogies, I think, are the religious movements which have occurred among primitives in recent times when their ways of life have been endangered, usually by encounter with the ways of civilized societies. Many of these happened in North America as the "Indians" there succumbed to Western colonization.[5] Some others occurred very recently in Pacific islands during the 1941 war with invasion of armed forces of the belligerents.[6] In these cases, charismatic leadership almost always arose, a leadership which was not often, if indeed ever, wholly reactionary, but instead sought to combine new practices with old. Although such new practices in these cases were mostly learned from the civilized intruders, they could presumably have been improvised out of untaught experience where there were no human opponents from whom to learn, as must have happened to the early settlers in the sites of the primary civilized societies; and those settlers who were not the earliest may well have learned some things from those who had preceded them.

Civilized man himself is just as prone to take refuge in religion when he faces utter disaster. In every decline of a civilized society a new or reconstructed religion, usually in several varieties competing with one another, has arisen. And that religion has quite obviously played a part in the revival of the civilized society or the rise of a new civilized society. The analogy with the rise of the primary civilized societies is clear and close. In a few rather exceptional cases of revival of later civilized societies the religion, or the predominant part of it, has been imported into the civilized world by primitives; the notable cases of this are those of the Greeks and

[5] See Wilson Dallam Wallis, *Messiahs, Their Role in Civilization* (Washington, 1943).

[6] See, e.g., Margaret Mead, *New Lives for Old* (New York, 1956), pp. 188-211; Peter Worsley, *The Trumpet Shall Sound: A Study of "Cargo" Cults in Melanesia* (London, 1957).

the Muslim Arabs. In all cases some material has been taken for the new religions from primitive sources.

In the civilized as in the primitive analogies cited, charismatic leadership was usually, perhaps always, present in some degree. That sort of leadership is also suggested by the evidence for every one of the primary civilized societies, even though by extrapolation backwards in time from later events. For the Chinese and Egyptian societies, we can make plausible guesses at the identities of some of the leaders, as will appear in Chapter 5. I therefore believe it is safe to conclude that the thesis proposed is upheld: every primary civilized society had, either at its absolute origin—whatever and whenever absolute origin may be thought to have been—or quite soon afterwards, a new religion, even if one constructed always in part out of old elements, and charismatic leaders who propounded it and played a large part in the early affairs of the society. If this is so, then it sheds a certain light of probability back upon the suggestions which have been made above about the circumstances in which the early settlers in the future civilized environments left their previous homes, the circumstances of their migrations, and the conditions they found in their new homes when they reached them.

How does a civilized society differ from a primitive society? Certain easy answers may be given to this question though none of them, nor all of them together, are more than a part of the whole answer. At this early stage of the enquiry only a quick, short inventory of the best known differences will be made. The subject will be taken up again at the end of the book.

The first easy answer is that a civilized society is very much larger than a primitive society, hundreds or thousands of times as large. It may be said too that it is more complex, but greater complexity is only a function of other differences, of which the difference in size is the main one. Some of the other differences are specifiable, and most of them turn out also to be merely quantitative: a civilized society gains more knowledge of the physical world than a primitive society does, and develops a larger apparatus of thought; it has more wealth in absolute terms, more per head of population usually, and so forth.

There are difficulties about most criteria which have customarily been used to distinguish civilized from primitive societies. It is not, for example, correct to say that all civilized societies have writing even if it is correct to say that no primitive societies have[7] (unless they have borrowed it from a civilized society, and such borrowings do not count in the distinction): the Andean Society had no true system of writing, and there were regions in the Middle American Society where there was scarcely a true practice of writing either. Moreover, writing appeared at very different times in the

[7] I think it is probably correct. Among the labyrinth of minor scripts— so far as I know—there is not even any probability of one in use among primitives having been developed there *ab initio* and without the influence of a model, or stimulus, emanating ultimately from a civilized source. Heine-Geldern has indeed argued that all (Old World?) scripts are traceable back to a people with gray and black polished pottery who lived in eastern Asia Minor and expanded from that region in many directions in the second half of the fourth millennium B.C. (R. von Heine-Geldern, *Paideuma*, IV, 1950 = *Mythe, Mensch und Umwelt*, ed. A. E. Jensen, p. 79). Heine-Geldern has no clear idea of the distinction between civilized and primitive societies, but by the criteria used here the gray and black pottery people were primitives. Heine-Geldern's argument on the subject consists, in any case, of a tissue of inferences, and it contains the notable flaw that the gray and black pottery people, who diffused their pottery to the Danubian primitives as well as to various civilized peoples, did not diffuse their supposed script to the Danubian peoples. I should only be prepared to consider Heine-Geldern seriously if his argument were transformed to suggest that the gray and black pottery people had particularly useful mnemonic devices, as mentioned in the text below, and that I should do only because Diringer and others have doubted the invention of a script actually in Mesopotamia (David Diringer, *The Alphabet*, New York, 1948, p. 41). I continue to think that the script as such *was* invented in Mesopotamia.

17

historic development of different civilized societies: in Mesopotamia it was slowly evolved in a period of small states when administration was no large problem, whereas in Egypt and Crete it was adopted relatively quickly at the juncture when the respective societies were being politically unified.[8] This difference reinforces the cases of the Andean and Middle American societies in showing that writing is not a necessity of civilized status, but simply an important device which may be used in a civilized society for various purposes.

If we seek to trace writing back to its origin, the search is likely to lead to mnemonic devices, to hunting-signs scratched on trees or stones, to marks on pots, to conventional designs made on objects marking places of assembly, and the like; and all of these are found in primitive societies. Almost certainly, it remains true to say that primitive societies do not have writing; what has happened in most, but not all, civilized societies is that one kind of thing, marks serving to convey simple information, has grown quantitatively until another kind of thing has emerged, and the quantitative change must be said to have turned into a qualitative change. This is the real significance of the occurrence of writing in most civilized societies and its non-occurrence in primitive societies. And, certainly, there are other practices and institutions which differ in the same way as between civilized and primitive societies. Perhaps indeed something of the sort should be said of civilized societies considered as wholes by contrast with primitive societies—but it is early in the argument to accept that conclusion.

The distinction which finds towns or cities in a civilized

---

[8] For Mesopotamia and Egypt, see H. Frankfort, *The Birth of Civilization in the Near East* (Bloomington, Ind., 1954), pp. 49-50, 105-108. In Mesopotamia writing was used early for "the administration of large economic units." For Crete, see J.D.S. Pendlebury, *The Archaeology of Crete: An Introduction* (London, 1939), pp. 118-119, 281. Cf. Diringer, pp. 41, 43, 54, 58-59, 72-75.

society and not in a primitive society is on much the same footing as the one which uses writing—until, as sometimes happens, its authors claim too much for it. There probably were no towns in primitive societies before civilized societies came into existence, although that is not a proven fact; there may have been some rather large villages, at any rate in the pre-civilized Near East.[9] From the Middle American Society doubt is thrown on the distinction from the opposite standpoint, for it is clear that in the Maya part of that society, which was the leading part of it, there was nothing which can properly be described as a town. But most civilized societies had towns and few, if any, primitive societies did. To go on from this to say that the substance of civilization resides in the fact that a society has towns is, however, claiming far too much for the distinction.[10] It is a mistaking of result for

[9] A spirited controversy (to put it mildly) has recently arisen between Kathleen Kenyon, the discoverer, and Robert Braidwood, with several others putting their oars in, about the status and dates of the early settlements at Jericho whose remains show no pottery (*Antiquity*, XXX [1956], 132-136, 184-197, 224-225; XXXI [1957], 36-38, 73-84). In the course of the argument, Miss Kenyon claims firmly that Jericho was a city and that it had at that time a civilization—and the claim is made quite evidently with some sense of what the terms mean (XXX, 187); Childe denies that it was a city, suggesting rather that it was a town (XXXI, 36-37); and Braidwood is apparently prepared to agree rather reluctantly that it was a town (XXXI, 74, 77). My position, on the basis of Miss Kenyon's report, is somewhat more skeptical than Braidwood's, which is already skeptical. Certainly, there can have been no civilization in the sense in which that word is used in this book. As to the town, I do not find that any of the items excavated there must have been town products, and would raise the question whether a good deal of the eight acres of walled-in land at Jericho was not really farm; in such a region inhabitants may very well have fortified themselves and all their effects against possible marauders. Not until the whole *tell* has been excavated can that be decided.

[10] I think it must be admitted that this is what Childe does. If he does not quite do it himself, certainly many of his readers get that impression from his writings. See V. G. Childe, *Man Makes Himself* (New York, 1951), pp. 114-142; *What Happened in History* (New York, 1946), pp. 82ff. I agree, however, with Frankfort, that in his last substantial treatment of the subject (*Town Planning Review*, XXI [1950], 3-17)

cause, and indeed of only one kind of result among many. A number of the villages of the early stages of development of a civilized society were destined to grow into towns, and they usually began quite early to manifest an urban character. Hence they serve well for diagnosis of the emergence of civilization, but in fact the civilization was in all cases present before towns appeared.

There is one distinction between civilized and primitive societies which is perfectly clear and is not only quantitative: civilized societies are all subject to a cyclical movement of rise and fall in the course of their development, but no similar movement occurs in the development of primitive societies. Rhythms dependent on the seasons affect all primitive societies, of course, but the cyclical movements of civilized societies are of millennial span. Sorokin has done more than any other scholar to show the importance of these movements.[11] He analyzes the cycle into three phases, distinguishing them in his own special terms. The three phases will not require close study in this book, but they will be called, where it is required to mention them, "age of faith," "age of reason," and "age of fulfilment."[12]

Childe moved in the diagnostic direction in his use both of the rise of towns, and of a number of other indices. Cf. *Antiquity*, XXXI (1957) 36-38.

[11] Pitirim A. Sorokin, *Social and Cultural Dynamics* (New York, 1941), IV, 138-142, 428-432; *idem, Society, Culture and Personality* (New York, 1947), pp. 584-634.

[12] Sorokin uses psychological-sociological terms: the "ideational" culture, the "idealistic" culture and the "sensate" culture. He considers the three phases to have happened in the development of Graeco-Roman and of Western civilization; I apply the concept to all civilizations. Three phases, stages, or ages have appeared in a good many other theories of history. Vico thought that in the history of every "nation" there were ages of the gods, the heroes, and of men, his nations being the Egyptians, the Greeks, and the Romans (T. G. Bergin and M. H. Fisch, *The New Science of Giambattista Vico*, Ithaca, 1948, pp. 301ff). There are several threefold successions in Comte's theory, e.g. the succession of three stages of the human intellect, the theological, the metaphysical, and the scientific (positive).

Two quantitative factors, both of them very great, are involved in this disparity of development between civilized and primitive societies. The two factors are a great difference in rate of change and a great difference in power of control over the physical environment. Many primitive societies scarcely change at all in thousands of years, whereas civilized societies do not remain unchanged even for centuries. Primitive societies, in general, can remain unchanged so long as their environment does so, but if their environment itself changes, they must adapt themselves to the change, or migrate, or perish. It is exceptional for civilized man to retreat before changes in his environment, though he has done so; he usually succeeds in adapting his environment to himself. Nor has any civilized society perished yet, either through causes arising in its environment, or through any other cause; at worst, it has been transformed into a new civilized society.

There is, then, in civilized societies a quality, absent from primitive societies, which impels both rapidity of development and domination over the physical environment and shows itself obscurely in the cyclical rise and fall movement.

We turn now to a different matter, an analytical examination of civilization.

In his Huxley Memorial Lecture (for 1945), Kroeber distinguishes between the style, or form, of a civilization, its cultural content, and the values it attains from time to time.[13]

[13] A. L. Kroeber, *The Nature of Culture* (Chicago, 1952), pp. 383-384 (The Huxley Memorial Lecture published in the *Journal of the Royal Anthropological Institute*, LXXV [1945], actually issued 1949, 9-20) ; cf. Kroeber, *Style and Civilizations* (Ithaca, 1957), esp. pp. 70-74. I think application of the epithet "national" to the styles in the Huxley Lecture is not the right use; the styles are styles of entire civilizations or societies, not merely of nations, which (in my terminology anyhow) are only parts of civilized societies. But this in no wise detracts from the value of Kroeber's insight into the aspects of culture.
Frankfort (*The Birth of Civilization in the Near East*, Bloomington, Ind., 1954, pp. 15-31) discusses the whole question of style, for which, how-

We shall not be much concerned in this study with values, for, even if these are inherent in a civilization from its origin, they are little developed at that time. With style and content, however, we are essentially concerned.

The style of a civilization is perceived as its aesthetic aspect; it is exhibited in everything the society produces and does, preeminently in its arts, but also in its thought, its politics, its institutions, its traditions, and in all its ways. It is possible to qualify a society's style, to comment upon it, to judge it even, yet hardly to describe it. It is the "Chineseness" of what is Chinese, the "Egyptianness" of what is Egyptian, the "Westernness" of what is Western. It changes with time and with place and yet remains always recognizable as the product of the same society. Those who get to know the style of any civilized society recognize it wherever they see it, for it is the mark of individuality of the society. Thus the fourteen civilized societies which have been listed above are distinguished from one another by their special styles. This is the criterion of individuation employed in this book, and all opinions and arguments which ignore, minimize, or deny this manner of individuation are rejected as wrong.

The cultural content of a civilization is what the anthropologist ordinarily calls culture traits or complexes, such practical traits as plowing, weaving, and pottery, such theoretical ones as divination, magic, and art themes, and probably many abstract and abstruse things which can be discerned by scholars only with difficulty. Culture traits and complexes can be diffused from one society to another, between civilized

---

ever, he uses Kroeber's alternative term, "form." Frankfort's idea of form is identical with Kroeber's idea of style, and I am quite sure Frankfort was, in fact, reproducing Kroeber although there is no acknowledgment; very possibly, Frankfort had forgotten that the idea was not of his own origination. Culture traits are present also in Frankfort's argument, and so is a concept of "dynamics," this last, however, not very effectively treated.

and primitive societies as well as between different societies of the same kind. Diffusion of traits between civilized societies has sometimes been taken to mean that the societies sharing a number of traits are parts of the same society, but this is only true when the style of expression of the traits is also the same in each case. In itself, the occurrence of the same, or similar, traits in more than one place has no bearing upon whether the same society exists in the two or more places in question. Each society inventing a culture trait, or receiving it in diffusion from another society, stamps the sign of its own style upon the product of the trait so that the products of different societies look different, unless perhaps for a very short time after a society has newly acquired the trait.

Diffusion can carry large complexes or small traits from one society to another. According to Kroeber,[14] it can carry a mere "stimulus" from one society to another, that is to say, a generic idea without any particulars of a trait attached. Diffusion can spread far by its two methods, migration of peoples and communication of ideas and practices. It can even be world wide, given a long enough time, though it rarely was world wide in the late prehistoric times with which this book is concerned. Often it is difficult to know whether the appearance of a certain trait in a certain society was due to diffusion or to separate invention, but, where there is doubt, I incline toward diffusion, especially in the case of any intricate complex or association of traits. Diffusion was never a cause or means of origin of a civilized society, but only a vehicle of its spread; that, however, is a rather special matter which will be further discussed below.

The enquiry so far, then, suggests that we learn little about a society from the presence in its culture of particular traits. Most traits do not even show whether the society is

[14] *Nature of Culture*, pp. 344-357; *American Anthropologist*, XLII (1940) 1-20.

civilized or primitive. Writing and towns create a presumption of civilization, but do not afford proof. As a rule, a particular trait or complex conveys, by itself, no information about a society which has it except its own existence in the culture. If a society is found to develop rapidly and to move historically through cycles of rise and fall, then the society is civilized. Any society, civilized or primitive, is to be identified by its style.

It must be supposed that at the foundation of the seven primary civilized societies the earliest cultural content was that brought by the immigrating settlers into the sites. It stands to reason, however, that the founders very soon invented a host of special practices, necessary to the novel kind of life they were developing in the sites they had found for themselves, and that these practices took a large place in the culture. Traits and complexes diffused from other civilized societies, and from primitive societies as well, were received from time to time, but there is no evidence whatever that any of the seven societies began as a mere colony, complete with culture content, style, and inherent or potential values, sent out by another civilized society. On the contrary, there is clear evidence that each society got started independently, for each one produced its own distinctive style, different from that of every other one, recognizably different even to a very moderately discerning eye. The independent start is confirmed for four out of the seven primary civilized societies by archaeological evidence of the immigration and settlement of peoples in the sites. Nor is inference of analogous immigration and settlement hard to support for the other three societies; it is almost certain.

There are certain false doctrines current about these fundamental matters. The doctrines destroy themselves when carried to their logical conclusions, and it is necessary now to bring the doctrines forward and let them show their quality.

One false doctrine is that of Sir Mortimer Wheeler which purports to find the origin of the Indian Society in Mesopotamia. It appears on first acquaintance an interesting doctrine, for Wheeler proposes that "ideas have wings"[15] and that "the *idea* of civilization came to the land of the Indus from the land of the Twin Rivers."[16] On examination, the *idea* decomposes into a series of different ideas, the idea of writing, of sealing, and others—only the bare idea being shared in each case by the two societies and all the details of application being different. We need not quarrel with this argument purely as an argument to establish a theory, for it is simply Kroeber's stimulus diffusion.

But Wheeler's application of the theory is quite wrong. His "idea of civilization," actually a very complex structure of purely abstract ideas all of them interrelated—and, as such, rather difficult to credit—he supposes to have been brought from Mesopotamia and planted in India precisely as from a mother country to a colony.[17] Such things have happened not infrequently in history, but when they have the colony has received from the mother country not only ideas and culture traits but also, and of crucial significance, the style of the

[15] "Archaeology and the Transmission of Ideas," *Antiquity*, XXVI (1952), 185.

[16] *The Cambridge History of India*, Supplementary Vol., *The Indus Civilization* (Cambridge, 1953), p. 15. (Wheeler's italics.)

[17] *Antiquity*, XXVI, 185; "Iran and India in Pre-Islamic Times: A Lecture," *Ancient India*, IV (1947), 91-92. Unwittingly, Wheeler defeats his own argument by instancing as a parallel Akbar's city, Fathpur Sikri, built entirely in Indian style, but embodying a purely Islamic idea (*Antiquity*, XXVI, 183-185; *Cambridge History of India*, Suppl. Vol., p. 15). The premise Wheeler fails to notice is that, when Fathpur Sikri was built, Indian civilization and style were already in existence and were by no means invented to clothe the imported Islamic idea. Contrast Stuart Piggott, who thinks it "inherently improbable" that the Indian civilization, as found on the Indus in prehistoric times, arose outside India; see *Prehistoric India to 1000 B.C.*, Pelican Book (Harmondsworth, 1950), p. 140.

mother country. Since Indian style is quite different from Mesopotamian,[18] the notion falls to the ground. It fails to account for the actual origin of the Indian Society; appropriately, but of course fundamentally, modified, it may well account for culture traits and ideas which came to India *after* the origin of the civilized society there.

Another false doctrine having a certain interest is Gordon Childe's supposedly materialistic doctrine. This doctrine allows the separate origin of the three valley societies—the Egyptian, Mesopotamian, and Indian—but then proposes that in those societies, under the government of kings or priests, surplus wealth was saved up out of the food produced by the peasants to become capital for all the economic purposes of a civilized society, one of the purposes being trade with other societies for the raw materials which were in all cases lacking in the valleys. The other societies, at first primitive, thus acquired an initial fund of capital for themselves and so were able to convert themselves into urban [civilized] societies. But "this," says Childe, "is not a case of like producing like"; as a matter of fact, Crete and other later societies differed more from "their reputed ancestors" than the ancestors differed among themselves. Moreover, the borrowing of capital by the later from the earlier societies "is most obvious in the case of cultural capital. Even today we use the Egyptians' calendar and the [Mesopotamian] Sumerians' divisions of the day and the hour."[19]

Cultural capital retains, verbally, a Marxist sound, but in fact calendars and the like are culture traits within the ordinary anthropological meaning of the term, while to say that the passage of cultural capital from an old to a new society "is not a case of like producing like" is rather a bland ad-

[18] As clearly recognized by M.E.L. Mallowan, reviewing Wheeler's book; *Antiquity*, XXIX (1955), 200.
[19] *Town Planning Review*, XXI, 17. Cf. other references in n. 10 above.

mission that borrowing of culture traits is not all that happens when a new society is formed—an admission, but no explanation. In fact, great as Childe's services have been to prehistory, this doctrine is not among them: it says nothing we do not already know and omits more of that than it includes. Moreover, the doctrine is not really in the hard currency of materialism: when cultural capital displaces financial capital, Marx is stood upon his head and Hegel hath his revenge![20]

Childe's doctrine does show, nevertheless, too great a deference to material things, for it is ultimately a doctrine which requires of necessity a certain physiography, invariable in its major features, for the origin of civilized societies, namely the physiography of great river valleys. In this book a strong probability will be set up that the physiographic factor was much more variable than this and, as a corollary, that the participation of the human mind in the creation of the primary civilized societies was the greater.

It is to be noticed that both Childe and Wheeler witness unwittingly to the soundness of Kroeber's discernment that cultural content is not all that is involved in the phenomenon of civilization. Childe does so when he admits that like does not produce like and Wheeler when he seeks to strip civilization down to an idea. Both obscurely perceive vital differences, but cannot conceive them as differences of style.

Robert Heine-Geldern appears—but for a single cautionary footnote—to think that civilization is in fact culture traits and that all civilization is one, having originated in the Near East of the Old World; the latter he certainly does think, whatever he means by protesting that he does not intend to propound so simple a theory as that of Elliot Smith and W. J. Perry.[21] Heine-Geldern has done some valuable work in

---

[20] "Though he claimed to be a Marxist, he was too great a man and too original a thinker to bear any sectarian label"—O.G.S. Crawford in *The Times* (London, Nov. 5, 1957, p. 13) on the occasion of Childe's death.

[21] "The Origin of Ancient Civilizations and Toynbee's Theories," *Di-*

showing diffusion from the Near East to China[22] and, some of it with Gordon Ekholm, from the Old World to the New,[23] but, in my opinion, he has shown nothing whatever about the origin of any of the primary civilized societies; on the contrary, he has brought into that problem only confusion.[24]

---

ogenes, XIII (1956), 81-99. The footnote of protestation is no. 33 (p. 98). The article is only incidentally concerned with Toynbee and in no wise succeeds in upsetting any of his doctrines—even if it ought to do so!

[22] "China, die ostkaspische Kultur und die Herkunft der Schrift," *Paideuma,* IV (1950 = *Mythe, Mensch und Umwelt,* ed. A. E. Jensen), 51-92.

[23] Heine-Geldern, "Das Problem vorkolumbischer Beziehungen zwischen Alter und Neuer Welt und seine Bedeutung für die allgemeine Kulturgeschichte," *Anzeiger der österreichischen Akademie der Wissenschaften,* phil.-hist. kl., XCI (1954), 343-357; Heine-Geldern and Ekholm, "Significant Parallels in the Symbolic Arts of Southern Asia and Middle America," *The Civilizations of Ancient America: Selected Papers of the XXIXth International Congress of Americanists,* ed. Sol Tax (Chicago, 1951), pp. 299-309. Ekholm's publications on the subject without Heine-Geldern's collaboration contain careful disavowals of excessive claims as to the significance of the material; see "A Possible Focus of Asiatic Influence in the Late Classic Cultures of Mesoamerica," *Memoirs of the Society for American Archaeology,* no. 9 (1953), pp. 72-89; "The New Orientation towards Problems of Asiatic-American Relationships," *New Interpretations of Aboriginal American Culture History,* 75th Anniversary Volume of the Anthropological Society of Washington (Washington, D.C., 1955), pp. 95-109.

[24] That the confusion may spread is shown by the reflections of A. V. Kidder as to whether the civilizations of the New World were independent of those of the Old: if that question could be answered, he thinks, "we would be well on our way toward solving the fundamental problem of whether what we call civilization arose but once and was passed from people to people, or whether it came into being among various peoples in response to an innate human urge, given suitable conditions, to take, and seemingly to take in more or less the same sequence, certain steps toward a better ordered and richer existence." (In R. S. MacNeish, *An Early Archaeological Site near Panuco, Vera Cruz: Transactions of the American Philosophical Society,* no. XLIV, Part 5, Philadelphia, 1954, p. 539, Foreword.) An "innate human urge, given suitable conditions, to take, and seemingly to take in more or less the same sequence, certain steps toward a better ordered and richer existence" is just the kind of omnibus conception which will not recommend itself to any critical thinker—and so will help to push the unwary in the direction of Heine-Geldern's thesis. The innate urge was quite certainly present, but it was

It is, in fact, not necessary here to pursue Heine-Geldern very far. Unlike Wheeler and Childe, he is not aware of differences of style, or he thinks them mere differences of detail not important enough to need explanation. His theory is an extremely simple one in terms of diffusion of culture traits alone. It is precisely the kind of theory which is proved radically wrong in subsequent chapters of this book.

Diffusion had nothing to do with the origin of the primary civilized societies, or of any civilized societies. The diffusion which brought particular culture traits to the primary civilized societies could have had nothing to do with their origin, for it occurred after their origin. The diffusion which was important to the primary civilized societies is the diffusion which occurred before their origin, spreading many mesolithic practices throughout the world and a number of early agricultural practices over large regions. In that diffusion the cultural virtuosity of the Near East of the Old World was of capital importance, but it had no direct bearing upon the

---

an urge only to survive; the rest followed without conscious human foreknowledge except in successive small bits, step by step. Of course, suitable conditions were present also, including the general similarity of the human mind from time to time and place to place, especially when averaged over populations of tens or hundreds of thousands and eventually of millions, but Kidder's phrasing may suggest, whether he is aware of it or not, that the alternative to Heine-Geldern's unity of civilization and infallible diffusion was either an urge containing foreknowledge in the human mind of all that would follow the first steps toward civilization or fore-ordination by deity.

Kidder and Heine-Geldern can, if they wish, find a demonstration of the same sequence of steps, not indeed between the Middle American and Andean societies, which every Americanist knows and which can be alleged (but should not be) itself to result from diffusion, but between the Mesopotamian and Andean societies, in *Irrigation Civilizations: A Comparative Study*, Pan-American Union Social Science Monographs, no. I (Washington, D.C., 1955), pp. 6-27. (Cf. A. L. Kroeber, "Summary and Conclusions," in Wendell C. Bennett, *A Reappraisal of Peruvian Archaeology*, Memoirs of the Society for American Archaeology, no. 4, Menasha, Wis., 1948, pp. 115-116.) I suppose that Heine-Geldern will argue that the successive steps were diffused from Mesopotamia, via China and India, to Middle America and Peru!

origin of civilized societies in the manner supposed by Heine-Geldern.

The mesolithic innovations of the Near East and the agricultural innovations both of the Near East and of other parts of the world will be examined forthwith in the next chapter.

MESOLITHIC AND EARLY

AGRICULTURAL SOCIETIES

FOR SOME ten thousand years or more before the emergence
of the primary civilized societies a portion of mankind had
been on the run before the worldwide climate change which
followed the last Quaternary ice age.[1] The portion in question
was that which had inhabited the Near and Middle Eastern
regions of the Old World, perhaps from as far west as the
Sahara to as far east as Iran. Those lands underwent progressive, long drawn out desiccation as the new phase of
climate developed, and the inhabitants introduced a whole
series of new modes of living in the course of their struggle
to survive. The new modes of living are those which scholars,
looking back upon the events, call mesolithic and agricultural.
In fact, these successive innovations formed an unbroken
series for the peoples who effected them, and only at the end
of the series was a climax of achievement reached which gave

[1] The time reckoned since the last ice maximum, Würm III, or a few
millennia later, the date of the maximum according to the astronomical
theory; see F. E. Zeuner, *Dating the Past* (London, 1946), p. 145; cf.,
more particularly for the New World, R. F. Flint and M. Rubin, "Radiocarbon Dates of Pre-Mankato Events in Eastern and Central North
America," *Science*, CXXI (1955), 649.

31

the peoples a certain respite.[2] The climax came with the evolution of a primitive grain agriculture, one of the very early kinds of farming, perhaps actually the earliest. This achievement put the peoples who made it somewhat ahead in the struggle they had been waging against the relentless physical deterioration of their habitat. How long the respite lasted we do not know, but it was not long after its end and the consequent resumption of the struggle that the primary civilized societies began to appear.

It has been said in Chapter I that primitive farming societies form the basis of all civilized societies, and so they do, but farming was only the climax of the mesolithic innovations, and farming societies incorporate in themselves the majority of the mesolithic discoveries, especially the craftsmanship of the mesolithics. These too are a part of the underpinning of civilized societies—as is very evident in the fact that most of our hand tools, even today, are mesolithic tools with iron or steel substituted for stone, bone, or wood.

Mesolithic and primitive farming innovations succeeded one another as a continuous series of adaptations to environment. Undoubtedly, they occupy and form a very special age in the human career. If there were earlier ages of the same general character, their achievements were so much less than these that they may be considered to belong to an inferior kind. Mesolithic and early farming adaptations show the art of adapting to environment carried perhaps to the maximum possible, and it is reasonable to think that, at any rate for some times and in some places, the practice of making cultural changes progressively to fit anticipated environmental changes

---

[2] The respite is shown by the relative stagnation of the main economic practices of the hoe-culture farm for a period after the hoe-culture level was reached. There were, no doubt, many earlier, and no doubt later, local respites due to local advantages, but nothing general in the Near Eastern region and in other regions adjacent; one of the adjacent regions was Europe.

became a part of the culture itself. To this sort of culture the culture of civilized societies offers a sharp contrast, not because the practice of making adaptations to environment was abandoned—although I suspect that it has sometimes become rather a rare resort—but because it has been superseded. It has been superseded, of course, by the new civilized practice of making the physical environment adjust itself to man.

A glance at the map of the Old World shows a continuous belt of deserts stretching from east to west across its northern hemisphere. The Sahara is the westernmost of them and the Gobi the easternmost. In between, from west to east, are the Libyan Desert, the Arabian Desert, the desert and semi-desert of Iran, the Thar in northwestern India, the Kara Kum and Takla Makan deserts north of Iran and India, and the Khirghiz Steppes north of the Kara Kum.

It was in or very near these deserts that the four river valley primary civilized societies of the Old World came into existence, and the deserts also had much to do with the preceding, long continuing emergence of mesolithic and early agricultural societies. But, especially in the matter of the emergence of those primitive societies, there was a great difference between the more westerly deserts and the others. The deserts themselves were not of the single, uniform origin that might be supposed from their continuity across the map. The common factor in their existence was the extremely dry prevailing wind blowing from the north across vast expanses of land and cold seas,[3] but apart from that they were very differently conditioned. The Gobi, the Takla Makan, the Kara Kum, and the Iranian Desert were cold deserts, perhaps a little drier, perhaps a little less dry at maxima of glaciation than at most other times.[4] The Thar is a mysterious desert,

[3] E. Antevs, *The Last Glaciation*, American Geographical Society, Research Series, No. 17 (New York, 1928), pp. 34, 39.

[4] Increased glaciation of high mountain ranges and extension of lakes

of whose history we know little.[5] All the westerly deserts followed an oscillation which is known, and was a greater one than that of the easterly deserts: the westerly deserts were always there, but at the really great maxima of glaciation they were substantially reduced in extent and, in what are now their less dry regions, they became savannahs, or, at worst, steppes. This is because they received the rain from the Atlantic winds which at present and in all interglacials pass over Europe and so miss the desert belt.[6]

---

certainly occurred at ice maxima in Central Asia, probably by reason of reduction of temperature and so of evaporation. But the extreme north of Asia was comparatively little glaciated; instead, the soil there was frozen hard and broken into very fine dust which the northerly winds, much stronger than in interglacial periods, blew southward and deposited as loess on the mountains and hills. The Gobi, Tibet, regions in western China and flat regions dividing the mountain ranges from one another in Central Asia contributed to the annual dust storms, but we cannot be sure how much they contributed. See Antevs, *Last Glaciation*, pp. 40-41; G. B. Cressey, "The Climate of the Glacial Period in East Asia: A Statement of the Problem" (Abstract), *Proceedings of the Third Pan-Pacific Science Congress, Tokyo, 1926* (Tokyo, 1928), II, 1818; G. B. Barbour, "The Loess of China," *China Journal of Sciences and Arts*, III (1925), 454-463, 509-519; reprinted, *Annual Report of the Smithsonian Institution, 1926* (Washington, 1927), pp. 279-296; Barbour in *Geological Magazine*, LXVII (1930), 465; J. G. Andersson, "Topographical and Archaeological Studies in the Far East," *Bulletin of the Museum of Far Eastern Antiquities*, XI (1939), 26-73. E. von Eickstedt (*Rassenkunde und Rassengeschichte der Menschheit*, Stuttgart, 1934, opposite p. 256) gives a map of the glaciation of Europe and Asia in the late glacial period. I think the areas there shown as periglacial cold desert should be extended considerably, especially in eastern Asia, and, if the period intended is Würm III, then the glaciation is too extensive; but the map gives a good conspectus nevertheless.

[5] F. R. Bharucha says that the Thar (Rajasthan) Desert is "mainly man-made" ("Afghanistan, India and Pakistan," in *Plant Ecology: Arid Zone Research*, Paris, 1955, p. 25), but there is certainly not enough evidence to warrant so strong a statement. The existence of the desert is undoubtedly related to shifts in the path of the Indian monsoon (see G. C. Simpson "The South-West Monsoon," *Quarterly Journal of the Royal Meteorological Society*, XLVII [1921], 151-167). The shifts may themselves be related to actions of man upon vegetation, but they are certainly related to other influences also, including possibly shifts of wind tracks further westward and northward.

[6] The movement of the track of these rain-bearing winds northward

The last ice maximum, the Würm III maximum, was not a great maximum, and its effects were not great either. Yet wide fringes of the westerly deserts and all oases within them became more extensive then than they had been. Thus the Syrian Desert, the northern fringe of the Libyan Desert and much of the Sahara had large territories at the time which were inhabitable for hunting and gathering peoples. When, therefore, the decline of the ice came and the rains were reduced and moved northward, all fringes of the deserts and all oases shrank, and the peoples who had lived in them were gravely endangered. The case of Iran, which contains the farthest west of the cold deserts, is different, but a recent study by Bobek shows that its waters were more extensive during the Würm III glaciation than they are today and, more significant, that it underwent some thousands of years of desiccation, becoming a good deal drier than it is now, within the period when the neighboring deserts to the west were losing their rain.[7] Bobek's dates for desiccation in Iran are from about 9000 to 4000 B.C. or longer. Desiccation thus probably began there a good deal later than it did further

---

and southward is simply explained in terms of barometric pressures: when the north Polar ice sheet was large, pressure over it was very high and it was quite high over all Europe except perhaps the northern Mediterranean coast and high as well over a corresponding latitude in western Asia. Consequently, the west winds from the Atlantic did not blow over Europe, unless at some of the milder maxima over the northern Mediterranean coast; they were deflected southward, dropping their moisture on the Mediterranean islands and on the Sahara, the Libyan Desert, the Syrian or north Arabian Desert, and to a lesser extent— lesser because of the amount they had already dropped further west—on the southern Arabian Desert. See C.E.P. Brooks, *The Evolution of Climate*, 2nd ed. (London and New York, 1925), pp. 55-74. The Würm III maximum being a minor one, the extent of deflection southward of the Atlantic winds was small, but it was in all likelihood quite important then within most of the area with which we are concerned, for the area is mostly within the northern latitudes of wind deflection.

[7] H. Bobek, "Klima und Landschaft Irans in Vor- und fruhgeschichtlicher Zeit," *Geographischer Jahresbericht aus Österreich*, xxv (1953-54), 21-25.

west. We know from other sources that all the cold deserts east of Iran underwent a drying process more or less at the same time as Iran did; previous to that time, however, they had for a few thousands of years become considerably wetter so that drying out there had started from a condition of exceptional moistness.[8]

The argument that there was still rain in this or that area at the juncture at which the civilized societies began to appear, or at some earlier juncture when advanced primitives did so, has little bearing on the experience the inhabitants of the desert belt underwent; it does not necessarily mean that life continued to be as it had previously been for them. The point is that, however much rain there was at this time or that, there was less than there had been earlier—unless it can be decisively established that, at some time or times, there were widespread reversals of the trend, and that has not yet been established[9]—and, if there was less than there had been, then the peoples living in the territory were under continuous pressure.

It was in these conditions of pressure in the Near Eastern region that the new crafts of mesolithic hunting and gathering and later of cultivation began and continued to develop. This was a simple chain of cause and effect,[10] and it began in the

---

[8] Von Eichstedt, *Rassendynamik von Ostasien: China und Japan, Tai und Kmer von der Urzeit bis heute* (Berlin, 1944), p. 27, n. 31. Bobek's evidence for Iran is all local geological evidence, and his only explanation of the phenomena the evidence signifies is one of a parallel development in temperature with the postglacial warm phase in Europe (p. 26). If the same major climate change raised temperatures in Europe and Iran, then it probably did so in the deserts further east as well, but the net effects in the three regions were very different.

[9] Bobek speaks of several oscillations between the arid postglacial period and the development of the damper conditions of today (pp. 22-23). He offers no dates for these and no explanation, and in any case, his evidence concerns Iran only and not the Near Eastern region west of it.

[10] Carl Sauer's pronouncement that the "saying that necessity is the mother of invention is largely untrue" and that agriculture "did not originate from a growing or chronic shortage of food" (Carl O. Sauer, *Agri-*

westerly deserts in which desiccation started earlier and was the more severe.[11] There is a certain possibility that some practices of outside origin were adopted, and adapted, in the Near Eastern region, but no possibility, in my judgment, that the main center of events was anywhere other than in the Near East—to be specific, in a region stretching from Syria-Palestine to the western scarp of Iran.

The main events were, of course, the invention of a long succession of new practices to enable people to survive. But, with these main events, there occurred a vastly important series of secondary events, namely the spread of mesolithic and agricultural peoples and their new practices literally in all directions and to every quarter of the earth. We are concerned here chiefly with one direction of that world-wide migration of peoples, the one which went eastward and northward.[12] Others, however, had their importance also; the migration into Europe, a territory becoming increasingly hospitable as the Near East became decreasingly so; the migration into tropical Africa which may or may not have been a large one; and, a probable migration into eastern and southern India and southeastern Asia.

The earliest migrants, we must suppose, congregated in the fringes of the deserts, especially in the mountains and in tropical forests where there was still rain. From the concentration in the mountains proceeded new events which we shall consider shortly. The main movement eastward and north-

---

cultural Origins and Dispersals, American Geographical Society, Bowman Memorial Lectures, Ser. 2, New York, 1952, pp. 20-21) is a gratuitous aberration of his own, and nobody else need pay attention to it. Cf. n. 29 below.

[11] See n. 28 below.

[12] The evidence of mesolithic remains in Sinkiang, Mongolia, and a good deal of Siberia (collected by Max Loehr in "Zur Ur- und Vorgeschichte Chinas," *Saeculum,* III [1952], 15-29) witnesses to the migration eastward in the Old World and to settlement of some of the migrants there for some millennia.

ward was the longest and most consequential of all the migrations. It was the longest probably because much of it occurred in the very period when the cold deserts were undergoing desiccation so that settlement in or near them could occur only to a limited extent. But we know that at some time settlement did occur in them, for the remains left by the settlers have been found. They are probably remains left by the early migrants who arrived before desiccation in the cold deserts had become severe. The migration probably did not at any time pass the Eurasian steppe north of Iran and the Kara Kum, and it is clear that for a good many millennia migrants did not enter North China in any numbers.[13] Instead, they moved on eastward and northward, picking up vast numbers of new peoples, mostly Mongoloid peoples, and continuing right across Asia into its extreme northeastern corner from which they passed on into the New World. Nor did migration stop at any limit there; evidently the pressure behind it continued. Ultimately both American continents were populated. The culture thus brought to the New World was basically a mesolithic one, even though new arts and crafts of kinds sometimes called neolithic or even agricultural followed, for it was the great mesolithic migrations which brought the New World its main human population.

There is a Mediterraneanoid strain among the New World peoples, and even the characteristic Armenoid type can be seen among the pre-Columbian American peoples and their descendants.[14] It is clear, then, that some of those who carried the mesolithic arts to the New World came from the region

[13] Loehr, p. 51.
[14] See the following portraits: J. Eric S. Thompson, *The Rise and Fall of Maya Civilization* (Norman, Okla., 1954), Plate Ic.; Sylvanus G. Morley, *The Ancient Maya*, 3rd ed., rev. by George W. Brainerd (Stanford, 1956), Plates 10d, 11a, and c, 23, all; 2nd ed., Plate 8c; *Handbook of South American Indians*, VI, Smithsonian Institution, Bureau of American Ethnology, *Bulletin* 143 (Washington, 1950), Plates 15 top right, 20 top left, etc.

in which those arts had been invented. But the Mongoloid strain is the largest, and this must mean a contact and mingling of Mongoloids and peoples from western Asia under conditions of severe population pressure, probably somewhere in cold Mongolian-Siberian territory north of China.

We return to the fringes of the western deserts of the Old World, in particular to the upland fringe of the Syrian Desert and the western scarp of Iran. There, where rain falls even today in quantities enough to support a considerable population, the refugees from the expanding deserts found their earliest stopping place even though desiccation was encroaching there also. It stands to reason that population congestion soon became serious; very probably it remained serious for a long time. The vast scale of the migrations northeastward of that first refuge (and northwestward as well) is a sure testimony to the pressure of population which grew up within it. Mesolithics in the New World reached maximum population density at .05 to .1 of a person per square mile.[15] Those were very highly skilled mesolithics; the level in the western desert fringe must have been lower, perhaps .05 as an outside figure, and at that level the desert fringe must have filled up quickly.

These are the circumstances in which cultivation developed in this area. It is not certain that cultivation actually originated there, although it may well have done so. The idea of cultivation and that of domestication of animals, which went with cultivation in this region, may, one or both, have been brought into it from a region far to the southeast.[16] What is clear is that the combined practices of cultivation and herding were either adopted or invented in the region and there developed into quite a new complex of culture, destined to

[15] V. G. Childe in *Town Planning Review*, XXI (1950), 4.
[16] See pp. 45-47 and nn. 29-31 below.

have a great future. The nuclear territory of this region, the territory in which the new complex was formed, was probably the middle elevations of the arc of mountains which sweeps northward and then eastward from Palestine through eastern Anatolia, Transcaucasia, Iran, Afghanistan on both sides of the Hindu Kush, into extreme northwestern India and into Turkistan.[17] Plants and animals native to those uplands entered into the stock of all the farming societies which grew up in the uplands themselves, and then spread beyond them in the adjacent flat lands and later far to the west into Europe and North Africa.

The uplands with the immediately adjacent foothills and flat lands are to be understood as a geographic unit in the early evolution of agriculture. This unit will be called here the western Old World agricultural region. The region came to have a large variety of leaf vegetables, root-vegetables, pod vegetables, and fruits. Its earliest important grains were barley and wheat, but it may well have had other grasses also at an early time. The region's animals were cattle, pigs, sheep, and goats. Dogs were, of course, a part of the assemblage, but they were not food animals. They had become attached to man early in the mesolithic period, if not earlier still. However important other vegetables and fruits were, the cereal grains were of greatest importance. It was upon

[17] In defining this region I have taken three "centers of origin" of cultivated plants defined by Vavilov and have combined them, his "Central Asiatic," "Near-Eastern," and "Mediterranean" centers (N. I. Vavilov, trans. K. Starr Chester, *The Origin, Variation, Immunity and Breeding of Cultivated Plants*: Chronica Botanica, No. 13, Waltham, Mass., 1951, pp. 31-37), but have lopped off all the western part of his Mediterranean center because we know that farming began farther east (even if the numerous garden vegetables of the western part of the center were taken into cultivation for the first time when farming reached it). So many of the plants Vavilov assigns to those three of his centers are repeated as between two or all three of them that it makes no sense to keep the three distinct for present purposes. But see n. 20 below.

them that man relied most heavily for his survival and, very likely, his domestic animals relied on them too.

The many different varieties of plants of the western agricultural region originated respectively in different parts of the region and the same is true of the far fewer different varieties of animals. Barley, one of the region's very early grains, may have been brought in from the outside, and, among its animals, the pig also. I am inclined to think that the easternmost end of the region, say, Afghanistan, northwestern India and Turkistan,[18] contributed a good deal less than parts further west to the total fund of the region. Both the vegetable and fruit lists for the eastern end as given by Vavilov, the Russian authority, are rather short. The eastern end had its own wheats, but they were of the complex forty-two chromosome varieties which belong to a rather late stage in the early breeding of the wheat plant.[19] I will, in fact, go so far as to suggest that the western Old World farming complex did not originate in the eastern end of the region, but was diffused to it from farther west in the region, a few new plants native to the eastern end being taken into cultiva-

[18] Vavilov's Central Asiatic center, more or less, but his centers are not defined in sufficient detail to make it certain where one ends and another begins.

[19] Cf. the wheats cultivated later in the Indian Society (of the primary cycle) which was adjacent to the eastern end of the region; Stuart Piggott, *Prehistoric India to 1000 B.C.*, Pelican Book (Harmondsworth, 1950), pp. 153-154. The origin of the forty-two chromosome wheats has been and remains a matter of speculation (see E. Schiemann, "New Results on the History of Cultivated Cereals," *Heredity*, v [1951], 305-320, esp. 314-315; Edgar Anderson, *Plants, Man and Life*, Boston, 1952, pp. 57-65, 163-164; J. Percival, *The Wheat Plant*, London, 1921, p. 339). They may have been a mere accident of cross-breeding of cultivated wheats of the twenty-eight chromosome varieties with *aegilops*. This accident, if it happened, could have done so at the eastern end of the region, but is more likely to have happened farther west. At any rate, no wild forty-two chromosome wheats have been found in Palestine-Syria-Anatolia-Transcaucasia, whereas wild twenty-eight and fourteen chromosome wheats are known there.

tion when agriculture arrived there.[20] I do not think it practical, however, to seek to limit the nuclear region any further than this.[21]

If the nuclear region of western agriculture was thus limited, it also had an extension of a special kind, an offshoot in Abyssinia.[22] It certainly had other offshoots as well, areas detached from the region itself to which its agriculture, together with domestication of animals, was carried across intervening spaces of desert or of sea.[23] The others which lie in westerly directions have no importance here and will not be considered, for no primary civilized society was specially related to them. But the Egyptian Society was specially related to the Abyssinian region, which, accordingly, must

[20] The proposed limitation is much the same as the limitation I made in defining the whole western agricultural region by lopping off the western part of Vavilov's Mediterranean Center, but there is no sure evidence that farming did not reach the eastern end at a fairly early date, and it almost certainly did so before it reached Italy and Spain.

[21] Ralph Linton refuses to make even a distinction like the one I make; *The Tree of Culture* (New York, 1955), pp. 92-93.

[22] Vavilov and some of his collaborators at one time regarded Abyssinia as the center of origin of hulled barley and of emmer wheat (*Bulletin of Applied Botany, of Genetics and Plant-Breeding*, XVI, Part 2 [1926], 154-162, 168-173; XIX [1928], 512-518; and Supplement No. 51, 1931), but in his latest work (see n. 17 above) the wheats are all given as subspecies, and so it is reasonable to interpret them as derived from species originating elsewhere. Schiemann elucidates this matter, showing that the wheat originated elsewhere and that the barley possibly did so too; see *Heredity*, v, 308-310. Cf. J. Percival, "Cereals of Ancient Egypt and Mesopotamia," *Nature*, CXXXVIII (1936), 270-273; G. S. Bhatia "Cytology and Genetics of Some Indian Wheats, I," *Journal of Genetics*, XXXV (1938), 321-329. A number of other items in the short Abyssinian list seem also to be derivative from the nuclear western region, so that it is only reasonable to see the entire Abyssinian Center as an offshoot from the nuclear western region of agriculture. This does not mean, of course, that no wild plants native to Abyssinia were taken into cultivation there.

[23] Braidwood evidently thinks the Maghreb territory of North Africa was such an offshoot, as well perhaps as territories in West Africa. He also implies that the Chinese region might have been an offshoot from the western region; see Robert J. Braidwood, *The Near East and the Foundations for Civilization*, Condon Lectures (Eugene, Ore., 1952), fig. 11, opp. p. 23. For the question of the Chinese region, see text below.

be considered. Egypt was settled rather slowly, and for a long period only by peoples who moved in from African territory further south,[24] Nubia or Abyssinia beyond it. These peoples brought barley and emmer wheat with them and raised them in the valley and also beside the Fayum Lake. But what clinches the argument is that they also brought sheep. It does not matter what kind of sheep they were; no sheep were native to Africa; they must have come from Asia.[25]

In the light of all the evidence there can be no doubt that primitive farmers, having barley, emmer wheat, and sheep, came at some time well prior to the rise of civilized societies and established themselves in Abyssinia. They would find there an upland country not altogether unlike the upland country of the western agricultural region, but they did not find much of it; the Abyssinian agricultural region is extremely small. Which way did they come? It is possible that they came from the Persian Gulf, coasting with a favorable wind, which they would get during a part of the year, all the way around the Arabian coast. But they could have come by land down either Arabian coast to what is now the Yemen and then across the Strait of Bab el-Mandeb to Eritrea. It is most likely that they came from, or via, Palestine-Syria and moved down the west coast of Arabia to the Yemen.[26]

The portion of mankind which had lived in the western desert region of the Old World during the last glaciation was

[24] It is now generally agreed that all the earliest peoples in Egypt came from Africa; see below Chap. 3.

[25] V. G. Childe, *New Light on the Most Ancient East*, rev. ed. (London, 1952), p. 26.

[26] Any primitives accustomed to living in upland territory who started moving south from Syria would be likely to go down the western Arabian coast, for there are hills all the way, and there are not hills all the way by any other route.

not the only one endangered by physical change when the decline of the ice came. All over the world the level of the oceans rose as the great accumulations of ice decreased. In some places melting ice, which did not readily find its way to the sea, inundated large territories. In other places there were great marine transgressions. One of the greatest of the latter was in southeast Asia and beyond, in what is now Indonesia.[27] There, the reduction of land space by the advancing waters caused sufficient congestion to drive the inhabitants into novel courses to survive.

It does not appear that the calamity in southeast Asia was at all comparable in severity with that caused by desiccation in the western deserts and subsequently in the eastern deserts of the Old World. To be sure, Carl Sauer thinks the mesolithic arts originated in the southeast, but there is almost no evidence to support that idea—and plenty, as we have seen, to support the idea that those arts arose in and about the western deserts.[28] In the nature of the case, the threat in

[27] The present Gulf of Siam, its extension across the South China Sea to Borneo and the Java Sea between Borneo and Java and for some distance beyond are not more than 100 fathoms, much of the area far less than that. F. P. Shepard and H. E. Suess have recently calculated an almost steady rise in sea level in the last 12,000 years from about 100 or 90 feet below the present level ("Rate of Postglacial Rise of Sea Level," *Science*, cxxiii [1956], 1082-1083). Their calculations are based chiefly on data taken in the Gulf of Mexico and off the coast of the Netherlands, two localities sufficiently far apart and free from special local conditions to be likely to give a reasonable guide for most other seas.

[28] Sauer gives five reasons for thinking that mesolithic innovations originated in southeast Asia ("Environment and Culture during the Last Deglaciation," *Proceedings of the American Philosophical Society*, xcii [1948], 74-75), but I can find possible substance only in the fifth, which concerns the origin of certain old domesticated plants, and of the domestic dog and pig. Even the possible substance in this fifth point, however, remains possible and not actual. It is possible that the dog and/or the pig were first domesticated in southeast Asia, but nobody really knows anything about this, and it is possible that the earliest plant cultivation occurred there, too—I do not, of course, object in principle to the implication that mesolithics were cultivators of, say, root-plants. Even if all these practices began in southeast Asia, however, and the first fish-hooks were developed

southeast Asia was a lesser one, for there was no important change of climate, and the encroachment of the seas could be seen, foreseen probably, and cannot at any time have affected such great areas as were affected by desiccation in the desert regions. There is no ground for thinking that there was ever any great exodus from southeast Asia as there was from the western deserts. But there is reason to think that the conjestion of population in the southeast was eventually enough to drive the people to cultivation, for a type of agriculture completely distinct from that of the western agricultural region and certainly of great age arose in this eastern region.[29]

It is, in fact, quite unknown whether eastern or western agriculture was the older, and whether one of the two was derived from the other. Their radical difference, the one based upon roots and certain fruits, the other consisting essentially and effectively of grain-raising, suggest that they were of separate origin, in which case the mere matter of priority is no great matter. In the last analysis there must have been a connection between the two since both were the work of

---

there too, I still think it likely that the development on a great scale of mesolithic hunting, fishing, gathering, and perhaps cultivation took place in the Near East and were spread far and wide from there; the evidence adduced above strongly supports this. And, as against even these concessions, it must be admitted that Sauer has an *idée fixe* about the originative importance of southeast Asia which does not inspire confidence.

[29] Sauer is, of course, an enthusiast for the origin of agriculture in this eastern region; see *Agricultural Origins*, pp. 24 ff. But he rejects the obvious influence of population congestion in bringing this about for reasons peculiar to himself; see n. 10 above. There are, however, some more serious advocates: Edgar Anderson (*Plants, Man, and Life*, pp. 142-144) gives direct support to Sauer's argument, not including his idea that agriculture was invented by people with an abundant supply of food already; A. G. Haudricourt and L. Hédin (*L'Homme et les plantes cultivées*, 6th ed., Paris, 1948, p. 88) reckon the plants characteristic of the region— without, however, identifying the region closely—as the earliest plants taken into cultivation; Ralph Linton (*Tree of Culture*, p. 95) regards the region as a "second and quite independent center of plant and animal domestication. . . ."

mesolithics, mesolithics having, in my opinion, moved southeast from the western deserts just as they moved in all other directions. In present knowledge the most probable hypothesis is that eastern agriculture was the natural resort of mesolithics in the tropics, where taro, yams, and other root vegetables had been gathered wild before they were taken into cultivation, and that western agriculture was, correspondingly, the natural resort of mesolithics in their original Near Eastern habitat, where many grasses grew wild and some had certainly been gathered wild before they were brought into cultivation.[30]

There is, however, a slender thread of evidence which suggests that western agriculture was derived from eastern and so that eastern was earlier than western. The evidence purports to show that barley, oldest known of the cereal grains of the western agricultural region, was taken into cultivation first in the central or eastern Himalayas, an area which was in touch with, or a part of, the eastern agricultural region.[31] It must then be added on speculation that the transition from root agriculture to cereal grain agriculture was made in the eastern region, a speculation rendered to some extent plausible by the facts that rice was at some time taken into cultivation in the eastern region and that wet barley cultivation, which appeared relatively early in North

[30] For example, by the Natufian peoples of Palestine, usually not considered as cultivators, who nevertheless made most elaborate sickles with which they reaped wild wheat (? and other edible grasses).

[31] See R. Freisleben, "Die philogenetische Bedeutung der ostasiatischen Gersten," *Züchter*, XII (1940), 257-272; "Ein neuer Fund von *Hordeum agriocrithon*," *Züchter*, XV (1943), 25-29; Schiemann in *Heredity*, V, 308-313; "Neue Gerstenformen aus Ost-Tibet und ein weiterer Fund von Hordeum agriocrithon Åberg," *Berichte des Deutsches Botanisches Gesellschaft*, LXIV (1951), 56-58. The theory is that *Hordeum agriocrithon*, a few grains of which have been found in southeastern Tibet and none elsewhere, is the wild ancestor of all six-rowed barley, two-rowed barley, wild or cultivated, being a "reduction form" of no genetical importance. Some of the grains mentioned were not found growing.

China,[32] may have been of eastern origin. Other supports are vaguer and weaker: that the dog and the pig were first domesticated in the eastern region, and that consequently the eastern region is likely to have been productive of other novelties also, including grain-raising.

But this thesis is threadbare in the extreme. The amount of barley which has been found in the Himalayas is critically small; nor was all of it found growing. The barley cultivated in North China may not in fact have been of eastern derivation. And, there is no compelling reason why pig and dog keeping should point to other innovations. We are indeed grossly ignorant on almost all matters concerning the origin of agriculture. We do not know that root-cultivation preceded grain-cultivation, or that planting, the characteristic practice of the eastern agricultural region, preceded sowing, the characteristic practice of the western region—although some scholars give opinions on these two questions.[33] We do not know whether certain fruits, leaf vegetables, pod vegetables, or nuts, were earlier or later than cereals or roots, or than one another. We do not know in what order manuring, simple irrigation, weeding, and selective breeding began—although there are various theories which relate to the order of origin of all or some of these practices.

What we do know—because this can be shown by comparative study of agricultures still practiced today—is that cereal cultivation was the greatest of the agricultural innovations. Whatever and wherever its origin was, it did far more for mankind than other cultivation did. It was essentially agriculture, and the great increase in human population which agriculture made possible, together with the respite which came to the inhabitants of the western agricultural region while the population was growing to catch up with the newly

[32] See below pp. 53-54.
[33] Some of these are given in n. 29 above.

available subsistence, must have followed as soon as cereal cultivation and sowing became widespread. If the western agricultural region had this practice first, then it attained thereby primacy in agriculture, whatever had happened earlier.

In another matter we know definitely that the western agricultural region attained primacy—domestication of animals. The eastern agricultural region of the Old World had only pet animals and animals kept for religious purposes, the dog, the pig, and fowls. These had little, if any, part in subsistence, little, if any, relation to agriculture. In the western region domestication of animals was in all likelihood secondary to agriculture. There is a little archaeological support for this probability now, but the old hypothetical argument that agricultural man could tame animals by feeding them with the surplus from his fields, at first perhaps only by letting them graze the stubble, remains important.[34] And this argument applies only to the western agricultural region, for only there were domestic animals kept in herds which would graze much as they had done when wild.

The agriculture of the eastern Old World region with its non-economic animals yielded relatively little to the peoples who practiced it, and it never became the basis for a civilized society. Those agricultures which did come to support civilized societies may be ranked, in the matter of domestication, from west to east with vast gaps between them. The western Old World region had, as has been mentioned, four food

[34] In two recent discoveries by Braidwood in the extreme north of Mesopotamia occurs a succession of animal bones which is suggestive. At Karim Shahir, probably a rather temporary establishment, "well over fifty per cent" of the animal bones were of "potentially domesticable animals." More than a thousand years later at Jarmo, a regular agricultural village, only five per cent were of wild animals (*The Near East*, pp. 26, 30-31). The distance of time is considerable, while, on the contrary, the area involved is not great. There can well have been variations from the time and the sort of succession in other parts of the western agricultural region.

animals, sheep, goats, pigs, and cattle. The Chinese region at first probably had only dogs and pigs. The New World had nothing until after civilized societies had arisen there and even then it had very little in either of its two societies. Ralph Linton has drawn attention to the very great importance of these differences.[35] They concern the sources of protein and fat in human diet, and, since man can survive without starch, which he gets from the cereal grains, but cannot survive without protein and fat, it might appear that domestication of animals was more important for human survival and for that great increase in human population which western agriculture made possible than cultivation of plants was. Actually, this was not so: first, because some plants, notably beans, also give protein and fat; second, because cultivation consumes much less time than gathering and so releases men for more hunting and fishing; and third, because the animals themselves live on the crops.

Yet these provisos leave western agriculture, with its associated domestication, in a very superior position as compared with the other agricultures. Indeed western agriculture increased its superiority to the others, for the western farmer developed the practice of dairying, which enormously improved his animal economy,[36] and dairying remained unknown in the other agricultural regions.

There is no reasonable doubt that of all the agricultures the oldest was either the western or the eastern agriculture of the Old World. We have, of course, no date for the beginning of either. The probability is, however, that both were very old.[37] It is probable, indeed, that the earliest agricultural

[35] "Crops, Soils and Culture in America," in *The Maya and their Neighbors* (New York and London, 1940), pp. 33-35.

[36] Linton, *Tree of Culture*, p. 94.

[37] Oakes Ames remarked that if man's accomplishments in plant amelioration gave a guide to measuring the length of existence of his cultures, then his cultivating practices would have to be dated back several multiples

practices occurred not long after the earliest mesolithic practices did and that mesolithic and agricultural practices were
so closely akin as to make it erroneous to distinguish the
two in the character of sharply defined successive eras in the
prehistory of man. We know, for example, of a crude irrigation practiced by mesolithics in western North America without any other accompanying act which could be described as
cultivation. This is the practice of damming small streams
and diverting their waters to run over places where edible
wild vegetation grows. Such a practice may very well go back
to early mesolithic times in the Near Eastern region of the
Old World, when refugees in the upland fringes of the deserts
must have had much acquaintance with small streams and
much need to improve upon the failing natural water supply
to the wild plants they ate.

As to dates of full development, we are no better off for
the eastern agricultural region than for beginnings. For the
western region we know that full hoe culture with sowing of
grain and the four chief domestic animals had been reached
by about 5000 B.C., and there is no reason to think that it had
not been reached a good many centuries before that.[38]

There is a possibility that the agriculture of the North
China region arose independently under pressure of desicca-
tion just as the agriculture of the western region of the Old
World may have done. The North China region at that time

---

of 500 years before 3000 B.C.; see *Economic Annuals and Human Cultures*
(Cambridge, Mass., 1939), p. 139. Even though they cannot be so directly
measured, the time required probably was very long.

[38] The Jarmo remains, which are of fully developed agriculture, have
been dated by the Carbon 14 method, from shell to 6707 ± 320 years ago,
and from charcoal in two places to 6606 ± 330 years ago and 6695 ± 360
years ago (Willard F. Libby, *Radiocarbon Dating*, 2nd ed., Chicago,
1955, pp. 79-80, nos. C-113, C-742, and C-743. The average is rather later
than 5000 B.C., but I suspect that the occurrence was during the period of
stagnancy in farming methods.

must be considered to have included Sinkiang, Mongolia, and some Siberian territory as well as North China proper—the easternmost of the eastern deserts and a good deal of land north of them besides North China, that is to say. At the time of origin of this agriculture large parts of the region which are now desert or steppe were inhabitable, and they became filled with mesolithics moving out of the western region. This movement was the great eastward and northward migration, and it must by its volume and long continuance have contributed greatly to population pressure in the North China region.[39]

Unlike the western deserts, the eastern deserts did not lose moisture from the beginning of the decline of the ice. There were many very great mountain ranges in the eastern deserts, and the immense annual melts during the decline of the ice produced a far greater summer water supply than at high glaciation. Consequently, for several thousands of years after the ice maximum the change in the eastern deserts was the opposite of that in the western deserts, which were losing the rain they had had. The extreme effects were felt in the lands adjacent to the eastern and northern mountains of Tibet, that is to say, North China and southern Sinkiang, which became heavily inundated.[40] The Yellow River, whose waters had been frozen tight at their sources during the high glaciation, now reappeared with huge annual floods far exceeding those of the great rivers of the west.

Summer temperatures had risen in the eastern deserts as everywhere else, but it was not until perhaps 9000 to 8000 B.C. that the rise began to overhaul the large supply of moisture.[41] At that turning point, to which there was no

[39] See n. 12 above.

[40] Loehr, p. 51.

[41] I follow Bobek's figure for Iran, but suppose that the change may have been a little later further east; the change was, of course, world-wide. Cf. nn. 8 above and 58 below.

EARLY AGRICULTURAL SOCIETIES

corresponding episode in the west, the water supply began steadily to decrease, continuing to do so until at least 2000 B.C., perhaps later. Lands which had been rendered inhabitable gradually ceased again to be so, while Sinkiang and North China dried first sufficiently to become inhabitable, but later gradually became less so, much less in the case of Sinkiang, not so much less in the case of North China.

In these circumstances, it is possible that cultivation began independently in the North China region but not very likely. If it did, it resulted at an early date from the great congestion caused in the region by mesolithics pouring in from the west,[42] or else, at a later date, both from congestion of population and from the net desiccation which set in about 9000 or 8000 B.C. The latter seems the more probable, but it is yet more probable that, early or late, some agricultural practices were brought into the North China region by the migrants from the west. And this last probability fits in with the supposition we have made that there was no sharp distinction of time between innovations which have customarily been called mesolithic and others which have been called agricultural. It would not indeed be worth considering the idea of independent origin of Chinese agriculture at all if it were not for the fact that, when we get to know it, it was so highly distinctive, quite unlike the other Old World agricultures. But Chinese agriculture is scarcely known until the time of the civilized society, and it may have been very different in its early days. Its early occurrence was almost certainly in Sinkiang and in the cultivable regions of Mongolia, including oases in the Gobi, but of that stage we are entirely ignorant, for no archaeological record of it has been found.[43] For all we know, it

[42] For the early date of mesolithic beginnings, see Sauer, "Environment and Culture during the Last Deglaciation," p. 73; but I do not hold with his idea that they occurred in Monsoon Asia.

[43] With the "Gobi neolithic" which has a crude, sometimes corded, pottery no indications of the type of agriculture have been found, but I think

may at that time have reflected western agriculture closely.

The later record is of agriculture in North China proper, which had never had a mesolithic population in the customary narrow sense of that term, but only a farming population which moved in when the land became inhabitable. That was after the desiccation in the whole region had gone on for a long time, had dried out North China sufficiently to produce cultivable land and had dried out the Gobi and Sinkiang severely enough to drive much of the population out of those areas into the newly inhabitable areas of China.[44]

There was then a grain agriculture, but none of the grains it used was obviously of western derivation. The ordinary millets (*panicum miliaceum* and other *panica*) and *kaoliang* (*andropogon sorghum*) are assigned in Vavilov's lists to China as their center of origin[45]—which may just as well mean some more northerly part of the region. Six-rowed barley, hull-less and awnless, another crop of the civilized society, which, as has been noticed above, was cultivated early in the region, does not look like a western plant either, for the hull-less and awnless varieties were planted wet, like rice. There was rice itself in early civilized China too—provided that the report of it from the settlement of Yang-shao-tsun is correct.[46] Rice, if there was any, must unquestionably have come from the south, the region we have called the eastern agricultural

---

it is this "neolithic," often showing association with the previous meso-lithic, which signifies the earliest agriculture of the North China region; for this neolithic see Folke Bergman, *Archaeological Researches in Sinkiang: Reports from the Scientific Expedition to the North-Western Provinces of China under the Leadership of Dr. Sven Hedin, VII, Archaeology, I* (Stockholm, 1939), pp. 36-37.

[44] For a consideration of their movement into North China, see Loehr, p. 52.

[45] *Origin, Variation*, p. 21.

[46] J. G. Andersson, "Researches into the Prehistory of the Chinese," *Bulletin of the Museum of Far Eastern Antiquities*, xv (1943), 297; Linton (*Tree of Culture*, p. 525) evinces doubt that the identification is correct.

region of the Old World, and hull-less barley is likely to have come from there also. Vavilov gives some bamboos, some fruits, and a few other vegetables which could be of eastern (southern) origin so that the question arises whether Chinese agriculture really derived from the eastern and not the western region of the Old World.

This question cannot be answered. All the evidence is late, and it may merely indicate late borrowings. But, after all, the agriculture of the eastern region is not a grain agriculture, and Chinese agriculture is. The issue thus reverts once more to the question of western derivation. Even wet barley could just be of western origin. More probable than that and more in keeping with the general view of agricultural origins maintained here is the migration from the western region of early grain-raisers with a crop of mixed grasses. The mixture could have included all sorts of things, even *kaoliang*[47] and *panicum*, for Vavilov's views of the origin of particular plants are far from decisive. More probably, it did not include *panicum*, but contained wheat and other grasses which did not survive in the northeasterly climate, while *panicum*, which may indeed have been a local wild grass, was brought into the crop consciously or unconsciously by the farmers and came to take an important place in it. But none of this argument has much ground. It may be said that Chinese agriculture probably borrowed plants or techniques from both eastern and western Old World agriculture, but in present knowledge there is no evidence whether one of those presumably older practices gave Chinese agriculture its start.

As with North Chinese agriculture, so with the New World agricultures, the question arises whether they were of original invention, or whether they were acquired by dif-

[47] Carl Sauer (*Agricultural Origins*, pp. 76-77) says that the cultivated sorghums originated in Abyssinia.

fusion from another agriculture, or other agricultures. If from other agricultures, then those were Old World agricultures, and this complicates the question: how could the practice, or the idea, of agriculture pass from the Old World to the New at the time when the New World agricultures arose, which must, at the latest, have been at some time in the fifth millennium B.C.? It could have come by sea across the breadth of an ocean, or it could have come by a short sea passage across the Bering Strait, or indeed by land from northeastern Asia to Alaska, for it is quite possible that in early mesolithic times, before the Würm III ice was all melted, a land bridge existed between the two continents.

Evidence exists to support both these possible modes of origin of New World agriculture, and to support separate invention in the New World also, but no one mode seems notably better supported than the others. In these circumstances, a summary treatment of them all is given here, and it is extended to cover the possibility that several of them contributed to the major agricultures which eventually emerged in different regions of the New World. Such complex origins are rather suggested by the apparently conflicting scraps of evidence which partisans of different explanations of New World agricultural origins propound.

It is known (and will be detailed below) that one of the major New World agricultures was well developed by about 4000 B.C. This was a grain agriculture, the maize agriculture of the Middle American region. There was also another early agriculture, the root agriculture of the region at present occupied by Venezuela and Colombia. There is no date for that, but it may have been even earlier than Middle American agriculture. All other agricultures in the New World are probably descended from one or both of these, and in such circumstances, if either or both early New World agricultures actually originated by diffusion from the Old World, that must have happened in the fifth millennium B.C. or still earlier. In turn, this means that the agents of the diffusion must have been primitives or virtual primitives, for at that time there were no civilized peoples sufficiently developed to have been appreciably different from primitives.

If, then, the earliest practice of cultivation was diffused by sea from the Old World to the New, this must be assumed to have happened by accident: primitives making a move from one place to another along some coast of the Old World must have been caught in one of the long distance ocean currents and thrown up eventually on a New World coast; primitives making a move might conceivably have stocked up their boats with sufficient food to survive the crossing and, more probably, could have kept roots or seed long enough to start cultivation anew in the new continent. Three ocean currents could have brought them: the Japan Current could have picked them up off the shores of southeastern Asia, carried them round the North Pacific, and ultimately deposited them somewhere on the coast of California; the North Equatorial Current could have picked them up off the northwestern coast of Africa or the South Equatorial Current off the Guinea or the Congo coast, and either current could have carried them across the Atlantic and deposited them on the Venezuelan-Colombian coast of South America or anywhere on the coast of Middle America.

The land, or Bering Strait, route, though the one usually considered by the few scholars who consider these hypotheses at all, is a far less likely route in my opinion—this, in spite of the fact that it was the route of passage of mesolithics (and palaeolithics, if any) from the Old World to the New. Mesolithic practices later to be consolidated with agriculture, such as elementary irrigation, could well have been brought by this route. So could certain "neolithic" practices, such as pottery—for today we have no difficulty in imagining the diffusion of pottery without agriculture, or agriculture without pottery. But cultivators taking any land route would certainly have attempted to settle, probably a good many times, on the way, would have found that they could not raise crops in the northern latitudes, would almost certainly have lost their roots or seed in the attempts to do so and have lapsed into fishing, hunting and gathering ways of life. Any other course of events is scarcely conceivable. It is scarcely conceivable, for example, that the migrants would have moved quickly enough to remember the idea of agriculture after they had lost the plants they cultivated. Their migration must have been a matter of generations, probably of many generations. Yet two speculative theories about this have been proposed, one not really offered seriously however, and both requiring fantastically rapid movement from Asia right into Middle America or beyond; these theories are not given space here.[48]

It is the long sea routes which are to be considered as possible, but it must be added at once that no vestige of Old World cultivated plants has been found in either of the two oldest agricultures of the New World. I do not consider that this tends to discredit the idea of a connection, however, for there is a real possibility that either or both of those agricultures began with plants different from the ones known to us. In that respect (though not, of course, in some other respects) both cases are on just the same basis as the case of possible relationship of North Chinese agriculture to the western or the eastern agriculture of the Old World. It is

[48] The theories are those of Carl Sauer concerning root agriculture (*Agricultural Origins*, p. 56) and of Eric Thompson concerning grain agriculture (*Rise and Fall of Maya Civilization*, p. 42). In the case of Sauer's suggestion we have to imagine the migrants hurrying all the way round from Malaya or India to the north coast of South America, and in the case of Thompson's suggestion all the way round from the northern limits of Asiatic grain—what kind of grain?—agriculture to the territory of the Mayas in Middle America—rather less far than Sauer's root cultivators!

also notable that the location of the New World root agriculture is very suggestive of African origin: either of the Atlantic currents would probably have deposited primitives picked up off an African coast on the very coast of the South American root agricultural region, and it is quite possible that Old World root agriculture reached Africa early.[49]

There is one piece of botanical evidence which suggests an Old World origin of a small body of New World cultivators. These are those very simple cultivators, whose remains have been found on the Andean coast and dated to about 2500 B.C.[50] Those people had cotton and bottle gourds (*Lagenaria*), neither probably for eating[51] and both of Old World origin.[52] This at so late a date need mean nothing at all for the origin of agriculture in the New World, but for one fairly obvious consideration: the people in question look like a marginal people who might very well have retreated to their inhospitable and then remote coast before the pressure of other, more successful peoples; if so, their ancestors in the fifth millennium or earlier might have come from southeastern Asia, where cotton was domesticated and bottle gourds were certainly well established, via the Japan Current and have been deposited on the coast of California. Cotton, as far as we know, did not reach Africa until a very late date so that the people in question could not have come over an Atlantic route.

In favor of separate origin of agriculture in the New World is, first of all, desiccation. This affected the region which is

[49] Carl Sauer, *Agricultural Origins*, pp. 34-36.

[50] See Ch. I, p. II.

[51] Bottle gourds were used for making cups, plates, etc. when the Spaniards arrived in the New World; see Carl Sauer in *Handbook of South American Indians*, VI, ed. Julian H. Steward, Smithsonian Institution, Bureau of American Ethnology, Bulletin 143, Washington, 1950, p. 506.

[52] George F. Carter, "Plants Across the Pacific," *Asia and North America, Transpacific Contacts*, Memoirs of the Society for American Archaeology, No. 9 (Salt Lake City, 1953), pp. 62-66.

today the dry southwest of the United States and northern Mexico. The work of Antevs has traced the drying process from a beginning about 8000 B.C. to a maximum reached about 5500 B.C. and sustained until about 2000 B.C.; the latter three and a half millennia Antevs designates the "Long Drought."[53] Even without the parallel—and the confirmatory dates[54]—for the desert belt of the Old World, it would be difficult to resist the impression that in this deterioration of climate we have the major physical cause both of the development of agriculture and, later, of the emergence of civilized societies, or at least of the earlier of the civilized societies, in the New World.

It could prove that an elementary practice of cultivation was brought in from Asia either before or soon after the effects of desiccation became severe, perhaps the elementary practice which has been found surviving on the Andean coast several thousands of years later. Or it could prove that root cultivators from the African coast were cast away on the shores of Venezuela-Colombia about that time and that some of their descendants moved north and took to grain agriculture under pressure of the growing drought. Or, something quite different, of which we get no inkling from

[53] In E. B. Sayles and Ernst Antevs, *The Cochise Culture*, Medallion Papers, no. XXIX (Globe, Ariz., 1941), p. 42, for the whole desiccation process and the pluvial before it; Antevs, "Geologic-Climatic Dating in the West," *American Antiquity*, XX (1955), 328-329, for a redating of the drought. Carl Sauer has recently argued that the last ice advance in North America, the "Mankato," occurred at a far lower date than used to be thought, that it reached its maximum only about 11,000 years ago; see "The End of the Ice Age and its Witnesses," *Geographical Review*, XLVII (1957), 29-43. His date is remarkably close to Antevs' date for the beginning of the desiccation so that it looks as if we have here cause and effect, and both Antevs' and Sauer's arguments are strengthened.

[54] Antevs' dates for the New World fit very closely with the dates we have taken for the eastern end of the desert belt of the Old World. Desiccation in the western end of the Old World desert belt began several millennia earlier by reason of the fact that there was at high glaciation a rain supply there and that that failed very early.

presently known data, may have happened. But it remains difficult not to think that the influence of the drought was the paramount influence upon events, just as was much more surely the case in the western desert region of the Old World.

We can, as a matter of fact, set up quite a good hypothesis from available evidence of how grain agriculture began in the New World. First, we know of alternating dry and wet spells in the Valley of Mexico.[55] This would suggest (though it does not prove) that local influences, probably of rains brought in on the well-known west wind from the Gulf of Mexico, periodically modified the effects of the drought in the valley and probably rather generally farther south. Secondly, the evidence for the beginning of grain cultivation in Middle America is now fairly satisfactory. We will consider maize cultivation in a moment, but there is also now the cultivation of amaranths for their grain to be considered. Jonathan Sauer has shown that grain amaranths are New World plants in origin.[56] The area of their cultivation included Middle America, and there is no doubt that they were taken into cultivation at an early date;[57] it is, in fact, unlikely that such a plant would have been taken into cultivation once maize had become an established crop.

As to maize itself, the earliest known remains of its cultivated forms have been found in Bat Cave in the San Augustin Plains of New Mexico; they date to 4000-3500 B.C.[58] But this region cannot be the region of origin of cultivation, for the plant is an upland plant, just as is true of the cultivated

[55] Paul B. Sears, "Pollen Profiles and Culture Horizons in the Basin of Mexico," *The Civilizations of Ancient America: Selected Papers of the XXIXth International Congress of Americanists*, ed. Sol Tax (Chicago, 1951), pp. 57-61.

[56] Jonathan D. Sauer, "The Grain Amaranths: A Survey of their History and Classification," *Annals of Missouri Botanical Gardens*, XXXVII (1950), 561-632.

[57] Carl Sauer in *Handbook*, pp. 497-498.

[58] Libby, p. 112, item C-573, 5931 ± 310 years ago.

grains of the Old World. I do not think there can be any serious doubt that maize agriculture originated in upland territory in Middle America, and this assumption is supported now by the probability that wild maize grew in the Valley of Mexico as long as 60,000 years ago.[59] The date of the beginning of cultivation must have been before the Bat Cave date, say 4000 B.C. or earlier.

It may therefore be proposed that refugees moving southward away from the area turning into steppe and desert land took refuge in the uplands of Middle America and there began cultivation of various grasses, including amaranths and maize, and that maize became the single most successful crop, analogous to both barley and wheat in the Old World. The New World grain cultivators may have invented the practice of cultivation for themselves, or they may have got the idea from peoples who cultivated other plants and whose ancestors had brought the idea of cultivation from the Old World. One possible source of the idea is from root cultivators established in the Venezuela-Colombia region of South America. It is very possible, however, that that was not the source, in fact that root-cultivation in the Venezuela-Colombia region was no older than grain-cultivation in Middle America. The movement of population southward from the steppe-desert region could very well have produced congestion not only in the broader territories of Middle America, where grain-

[59] I am grateful to Professor Junius Bird for his warning (oral communication) that the evidence to support this (which follows) may not be taken as final. As a matter of fact, I have been satisfied of the Middle American origin of maize since the work of Vavilov on the subject. The main recent material is: E. S. Barghoorn, M. K. Wolfe, and K. H. Clisby, "Fossil Maize from the Valley of Mexico," *Botanical Museum Leaflets*, Harvard University (Cambridge, Mass., 1954), XVI, 229-240; concurrence, C. Mangelsdorf, "New Evidence on the Origin and Ancestry of Maize," *American Antiquity*, XIX (1954), 409-410; L. F. Randolph, "Cytogenetic Aspects of the Origin and Evolutionary History of Corn" in *Corn and Corn Improvements*, ed. G. F. Sprague (New York, 1955), pp. 53-55.

raising began, but also on beyond the isthmian territories, which could hold little population, in the Venezuela-Colombia region. Such a congestion in that region may have led to the emergence of root agriculture there, just as a congestion caused in another way may have led to the emergence of a different root agriculture in the eastern agricultural region of the Old World.

Middle American agriculture was the earliest of the New World grain agricultures, as has been mentioned. The northern boundary of the Middle American agricultural region must have been somewhere in north-central Mexico, in high country since all its important vegetables, not only the grains, were of upland origin, just as was the case in the western region of the Old World. To delimit the region southward is more difficult, for the climate and physiography continue to be suitable right into Costa Rica at least. But the chief crops certainly originated in Middle America itself. Maize, beans, and gourds (*Cucurbita*) were cultivated together there on small heaped-up mounds of earth, a practice quite unlike any Old World grain raising practice, but, significantly, related to the planting practice in the root agriculture region of the New World to the south.[60] There were also jack beans and a number of fruits and miscellaneous items. There were no domestic animals. The stock was vastly smaller than those of the Old World regions which have been considered, but certain important borrowings were made from South American regions later, and the turkey was domesticated at some time.

The other New World grain agriculture with which we are concerned is that of the western South American region. The limits of this region are as hard to define northward as those

[60] Carl Sauer, *Agricultural Origins*, cf. pp. 45 and 70.

of the Middle American region are southward. The two may well have been continuous, but the western South American region is entitled to some degree of separate individuality, for it originated a number of distinct new cultivated plants. Southward, the region is rounded off by climate in Bolivia, and its nuclear territory covers all the middle elevations of the Andes within this extent, and, for a few vegetables, elevations higher than middle.

Undoubtedly, there was land undergoing desiccation nearby the region at the time when agriculture began there. The coastal desert had certainly been in existence for a long time, and its fringes were, no doubt, moving outwards as the water supplies from annual melts in the Andes got less. But there had probably not been room there, even at the height of the last glaciation, to accommodate much of a population. Hence, when that population, if any, had to move, it might have found place for itself in the upland regions. Such broader areas as the Sechura Desert in northern Peru and the Atacama Desert at the southern end of the region are perhaps more likely sources of a population driven to move, but even this cannot have been a very large population. No doubt, too, there were plenty of peoples already living in upland territory who found their water supplies decreasing.

But the difficulty in discovering local conditions in the western South American region sufficient to drive men to cultivation is that there was too ample a refuge from want for them near at hand. Over the high mountains on their eastern slopes tropical forest began, and those who could get that far must certainly have been able to find sustenance without taking to desperate experiments. There is not the least probability that that region was fully inhabited. Even the mountains themselves were probably not filled with a hunting and gathering population if the scanty archaeological explorations which have been made there are an adequate guide.

And, little as we know about early agriculture in the western South American region, that little carries at least a few broad hints that agriculture was imported there from the Middle American region. We have already supposed that the earliest agricultural settlers on the Peruvian coast were marginal peoples who had been pushed southward by others. If so, they brought their simple agriculture with them from some older agricultural region farther north. Pottery and, soon after it, maize came to these peoples, possibly by the intrusion of other peoples, towards the end of the second millennium B.C. A grain agriculture complex was then fully established in the western South American agricultural region. This strongly suggests that the agriculture of the region was derived from that of the Middle American region. And this is no surprise, for such a relationship with an older New World region is logical in view of the absence of evidence of compulsion upon man in the western South American region to find himself new food resources or perish.

We know little more than this, however, about the origin of agriculture in the western South American region. The region came to have a small, but fully adequate, collection of vegetables, of which the most famous is undoubtedly the potato. Many varieties of potato were grown in the high Andes, even in the very high Andes. The wild potato had flourished, and still does, from Central America to as far south as Bolivia.[61] The region came also to have two domestic animals, the llama and the alpaca, but these were not eaten, except in very small numbers in religious ceremonials.

The earliest settlers on the Andean coast, who have played an important part in the present enquiry, need not have been the earliest cultivators in the western South American region, but they may have been. Even if they were not, there is no

[61] Vavilov, *Origin, Variation*, p. 41.

reason to suppose that agriculture was earlier there than about 3000 B.C.

This completes the survey of the origin of seven of the world's early agricultures, the five grain agricultures which were subsequently involved in the origin of the seven primary civilized societies, and two root agricultures which may, but again may not, have been involved in the origin of the grain agricultures.

In only two cases is a derivative relation firmly ascribed to pairs of the seven agricultures: it is proposed that Abyssinian agriculture was derived from western Old World agriculture and that western South American agriculture was derived from Middle American agriculture. In each of these two cases the younger agriculture owed its characteristic grain crop and, no doubt, other crops to the older agriculture. If it seems likely that North Chinese agriculture owed something to both the western and eastern Old World agricultures, it is quite unsure whether it owed its origin to either and sure that it did not owe to either its characteristic grain crops. It is also quite unsure whether the leading grain agricultures of the Old and New Worlds, western Old World agriculture and Middle American agriculture, owed their origin to the respective root agricultures, or vice versa, or whether the root and grain agricultures originated independently of one another. Finally, whether there were relations between New World and Old World agricultures remains not only unsure, but confused and even contradictory in present knowledge.

My personal opinion is that, when, if ever, sufficient reliable evidence about relationships comes to hand, it will show in most cases some debts as between the various regions and types, including debts of the New World agricultures to the Old World agricultures. This does not mean, of course, debts *after* origins; such debts are already well proven and are likely

65

to seem commonplace as knowledge increases. Nor does it mean debts of such main substance as staple crops. It means debts actually *at* origins of ideas, of elementary practices which could be superseded by more effective ones and perhaps of practices and plants suited to one region but not to the particular borrowing region. I imagine that mesolithics employed in their food-getting many elements of agriculture which the archaeologist does not detect in their remains—he does detect some—and that some of the differences between the early agricultures are explained by debts to those elements rather than by direct debts to one another.

If this is really the nature of the relations between the different early agricultures, then there remains an impressive similarity between the development of the root agricultures of the Old World and the New, between the development of the three earliest—original?—grain agricultures, the similarity of the succession of grain agriculture to root agriculture or vice versa in two instances, or alternatively, the similar separate emergence of root and grain agricultures in the two instances. These similarities can by no means have been wholly determined by the tenuous original relationships between the different agricultures. Neither can they have been caused by similarities of environment alone, nor by the "psychic unity of mankind."[62] But the generally similar mentality of men—hardly the "psychic unity"—similar environment, similar changes in environment, and intrinsic continuities of functional development beginning with the original relationships: these factors, taken together, may well explain the repetitions in the origin and development of the early agricultures.

[62] Carl Sauer decries the "psychic unity of mankind" and also the power of environmental influences. Another, much milder, skeptic is A. V. Kidder; see Ch. 1, n. 24. I think the belief in invariable and unmixed diffusion is just as naive as the belief in unvarying repetition of the same evolutionary succession in independent instances.

THE RIVER VALLEYS

FIVE of the narrow territories in which primary civilized societies originated were the valleys of rivers. The five societies were the Egyptian, Mesopotamian, Indian, Chinese, and Andean societies. Deterioration of climate by desiccation was in all five cases the ultimate cause of the resort of peoples to the river valleys. But two other causal factors contributed to impel the peoples to move: one was their increase in numbers and the other their exhaustion of the soil in the regions where they had been living. Both these factors may be considered secondary to desiccation in the sense that they were incidental to farming and that farming, as we know, was developed by man as a part of his earlier defence against desiccation. All three factors—increase of population, wastage of soil and continuing desiccation—operated closely and intimately together to drive humanity relentlessly out of country which had once been a safe refuge.

The increase in numbers was made possible by the vastly increased supplies of food which farming and stock-keeping afforded. It was, of course, the increased supplies which had given humanity its respite in the struggle with the climate, and the increase in human population is the decisive evidence that the respite occurred. But increased numbers were positively attractive to primitive farmers besides being merely possible : they gave more hands on the farm, for even children could make themselves useful there, and they gave strength against enemies, against human enemies chiefly, no doubt, but also against dangerous predatory animals. It may be assumed that primitive farmers, when they began the practice of increasing their families, knew nothing of the congestion to which the increase must eventually expose them. This they must have found out when the practice had become a part of the culture, well established and difficult to break or to curb. Nor indeed can its inherent danger, which is impalpable and not immediately obvious, have wholly outweighed its real advantages.

As to waste of the soil, there is no evidence that the primitives of precivilized times ever tried to do anything about it except to move on to new soil. There is, in fact, so much evidence that they did that and did it repetitively and rapidly, that the presumption arises that they made no attempts at all at conservation, or none which took appreciable effect. As has been said in Chapter 1, the effect of soil wastage must have varied a good deal with the variation of the initial quality of the soil in different farming regions and perhaps too with the relative wastefulness of different farming methods; but all methods known to the farmers of all the different farming regions at the time were very wasteful.

Desiccation continued its millennial process. Just as when agriculture originated, so when civilized societies did so, the effect of desiccation was felt later in the New World than in the western part of the Old World. In the northeastern part of the Old World the crisis came later than it did in the western part. These differences were due in the main to differences in the time of the physical changes in the three parts of the world in question. As between the two parts of the Old World, however, movement of population was also a factor:

refugees in the western agricultural region not only sought the great river valleys of that region; some of them moved eastward into the North China region and before long were involved there in the resort to North China proper, the basin of the Yellow River, where the Chinese civilized society arose.

The crisis which led to the creation of civilized societies was, as far as we can tell, very much the same in each region. In the western agricultural region it produced four different civilized societies, the Egyptian, Mesopotamian, Indian, and Cretan societies, whereas in the three other regions it produced only one each. This may be because western Old World agriculture and stock-keeping had led to a greater increase in population than the other agricultures had. But it cannot be said that we know this; alternative refuges may have been fewer and less easily accessible to peoples in the western Old World region; I rather think they were. We do not know the relative importance of the three factors, population increase, soil wastage, and desiccation itself in the four regions. We may guess perhaps, from what is shown about religion in Chapter 5, that desiccation in all cases *appeared* to the respective peoples to be the one great danger. There is no sign that any of them tried to meet the population pressure by abortion, or birth control, as some historical primitives have done. Very possibly the special fertility and the annual renewal of the soils in the river valleys, which in effect wholly neutralized soil wastage, was a fortunate accident, but it may not have been; the refugees may have discovered it before they sought refuge in the valleys. I think the refugees probably knew of the existence of the valleys for a long time before they moved into them—that they did not merely stumble upon them in desperate flight. But in no case was a river valley in itself attractive: every valley presented formidable difficulties as a habitat for farming peoples, and that, no doubt, is why farming peoples had not settled in them

69

much earlier. Apart from floods, the valleys were at all times filled with swamps. They were overgrown with rank vegetation which was extremely difficult to clear out, but had to be cleared out if there were to be sufficient fields for cultivation.

Scholars have found places which still show today the physical conditions of some of the valleys before man subdued them. The Nile of that time is reflected, on a wider scale, in the southern Sudanese swamp country of the Bahr-el-Ghazal. The Tigris and Euphrates valleys, on the contrary, are represented in their pristine condition, but on a narrower scale and even wetter than they were, in the marsh lands which spread out from the Shatt-el-Arab where that channel carries the waters of both rivers to the Persian Gulf.[1] The lower Yellow River valley, as it was at the time of settlement, is reflected still in the upper valley of the Ussuri, a tributary of the Amur on the eastern frontier of Manchuria.[2]

In the case of the Nile there is literary confirmation of this ancient physiography and archaeological confirmation in reliefs left from early historical times, when some wild country still survived in the valley.[3] The former gives descriptions of hunts in the valley swamps, the latter shows birds and animals found today only on the high tributaries of the river. Similarly, the early state of the Indus is well indicated by a wet-country fauna, now long disappeared, portrayed in pictorial remains at Mohenjo-daro.[4]

[1] Lees and Falcon's demonstration of the geological character of lower Mesopotamia makes it possible that the country of the Shatt-el-Arab has become today swampier than any part of the lower valley was in the fifth and fourth millennia B.C., but not, I believe, that the valley was not swampy at all. See G. M. Lees and N. L. Falcon, "The Geographical History of the Mesopotamian Plains," *The Geographical Journal*, CXVIII (1942), 24-39.

[2] Toynbee gives good accounts of conditions on the Nile, the Tigris and Euphrates, and the Yellow River; *A Study of History*, I (London, 1934), 303-321. See also the authorities he quotes.

[3] See John A. Wilson, *The Burden of Egypt* (Chicago, 1951), fig. 2a between pp. 76 and 77.

[4] Sir John Marshall, *Mohenjo-daro and the Indus Civilization*, I (London, 1931), 2.

It was a formidable task for primitive farmers to establish themselves in wild, swamp-filled country of this kind. The annual inundation alone was a threat to their existence, and their earliest settlements were almost always confined to land beyond the widest reach of the inundation, land which was also more or less free of swamps, but by no means free of powerful reed coverings. The amount of that land which was wet enough to raise crops varied much in different cases. It was always good land, but it was subject to the unremitting desiccation everywhere in progress, and after a while it would be exhausted by the settlers' methods of cultivation. Eventually, then, in all cases the settlers had to move into the swampland itself. It is worth noticing that, when they had to do so, both the swamps and the inundations had become less than they had been at any time previously during the existence of agricultural man. The desiccation which had driven the settlers from their old homes and then from such temporary refuges as they had found beyond the swampland was also steadily reducing the annual floods and the swamps in the inner valleys. A certain gradualness is, in fact, sure in the movement of the settlers into the inner valleys; they were at first drawn by shrinkage of the waters as well as driven by shrinkage of their temporary refuges. Presumably, they had soon to undertake draining and diking operations.

However those tasks were accomplished, the accomplishment, when made, was in every case a triumphant success. It gave a final solution of the water problem, and at the same time it gave a solution of the problem of soil wastage, for the inundation brought each year a new soil cover in the alluvium it carried so that the land became literally inexhaustible and fantastically fertile as well; only it was necessary to learn first how to let the inundation cover the land, how to remain safe from it and to keep animals and goods safe from it, and how to cause the fertilizing waters to withdraw after they had done their work and to leave the fields free for sowing.

71

Even the population problem was solved for a long time—for a time long enough to permit the civilized societies to grow up and to find entirely new ways of enlarging the material resources available to sustain the human species.

The material conditions at the origin of each of the valley societies will now be reviewed seriatim, those for Egypt being taken first. The sources of the data are three, archaeological, geological, and mythological. The two former are the usual data used in studies of the origin of civilized societies, and they will be supplemented, also in the usual manner, by such later literary data as may have bearing upon origins. The mythological data will be employed not only in this chapter, but throughout the remainder of the book. It is my opinion that this source of information has not been sufficiently exploited.[5] In this chapter the myths to be used are mainly creation myths.

[5] It is necessary to deal carefully with mythological evidence. Myth is in its nature cumulative, repetitive, and constructive rather in the baffling manner that dreams are, and beyond that it is subject often to reshaping for ecclesiastical-political purposes by priests. Some of the substance of the myths with which we shall be concerned is an inheritance from primitive times before the rise of civilized societies; that, however, is not hard to detect, and besides it has its special use here. Confusion may arise occasionally from the entry of new myth into the "conglomerate myth" (for the term, see my "Concept of the 'Conglomerate Myth': A Speculative Thesis concerning the Place of Religion in History," *Proceedings of the Tenth International Congress of Philosophy*, ed. Beth, Pos and Hollak, I, Amsterdam, 1948, pp. 761-768) which is formed every time a civilized society revives after a decline. Such new myth may be from many—it may almost be said any—source, civilized or primitive. It becomes necessary to trace carefully the pedigree of any myth found at a late date in the record of a civilized society. The fact that mythology similar to that found in civilized materials turns up fairly often in the materials of primitive societies surviving today is nothing to worry about; it has in such cases been diffused to the primitive societies from civilized sources.

For the value of mythological material, cf. J. H. Breasted, "Historical Tradition and Oriental Research," *Annual Report of the Smithsonian Institution, 1924*, pp. 413, 414.

All Egyptian creation myths we know begin with chaos and the primordial waters. One myth tells of the god who was in himself the land rising from the waters, another of the god, in whose image man was made, providing for man's needs by driving away the water monster. Several myths hypostatize the primordial waters as the goddess Nūn from whose substance life first came. Another myth gives a "primeval hillock" upon which Atum, the sun-god, created himself and thereafter created the rest of the universe.[6] Henri Frankfort, in his general survey of the origins of civilization in the Near East, argues that some of the very earliest settlements in the Nile valley were made on hillocks in the midst of the swamp.[7] Such hillocks, he thinks, were formed as banks of the river by deposit of silt and by catching windblown dust; but after a time the river would break through the bank so formed and find a new course in the lower lying land beyond it, leaving the old course as swampland and the bank as a series of hillocks standing above both river and swamp.[8]

Frankfort goes on to say, "All traces of these settlements in the valley proper have long since disappeared; they have been not merely silted over but washed away by the changes in the river's course. This explains why we find traces of early settlements only at the edge of the valley, on the spurs of detritus at the foot of the high cliffs [cliffs at which the high desert ends and the valley depression begins]."[9] Frankfort, then, believes that, although there is now no evidence of early settlements right in the valley, such settlements were made, and that the earliest settlements of which we do have

[6] Wilson, in H. and H. A. Frankfort, John A. Wilson, Thorkild Jacobsen, and William A. Irwin, *The Intellectual Adventure of Ancient Man* (Chicago, 1946), pp. 45-55.

[7] *The Birth of Civilization in the Near East*, p. 41.

[8] Frankfort does not say whether he had the myths in mind when he propounded his opinion, but I should not be surprised if he had.

[9] *Birth of Civilization*, p. 41.

73

archaeological evidence were not the only very early settlements.

As to the settlements of which we have record, there are two groups of them, one in the north, the region known as Lower Egypt, and the other to the south, on the middle course of the Nile, in the region of Upper Egypt. One of the two settlements of the northern group was outside the valley altogether. It was beside the Fayum Lake, the large lake which once existed on the west side of the river, about twenty-five miles from it and some 130 miles from the present coast of the delta.[10] There was on the northwestern shore of the Fayum Lake a large, scattered village, or possibly a group of small, closely related villages. Over fifty miles farther north was another village, near the modern Merimde-Beni-salame, lying a little more than a mile from where the Rosetta branch of the delta flows today.[11]

The other group of earlier settlements is known from remains scattered along the east side of the river, at the outer edge of the valley, between the outer margin reached by the inundation and the cliffs where the high desert ends. It runs from the region of the (modern) villages of Khawaled and Deir Tasa past Badari to Hammamiya. The distance overall is some thirty-five miles. Most of the remains found are of cemeteries, but there are a few of village or camp settlements also. The location is far from that of the first group, the nearest "Badarian" remains, as they are called, being more than 150 miles from the Fayum settlements. The cultural

[10] The existing Birket Qarun is a very much shrunken survival of the Fayum Lake.

[11] It has not been usual in recent years to include the settlements beside the Fayum and near Merimde-Benisalame among the original settlements of farming peoples in Egypt; cf. Elise Baumgartel, *The Cultures of Pre-historic Egypt* (London, 1947), pp. 14-18; Frankfort, *Birth of Civilization*; and A. H. Brodrick, *The Tree of Human History* (New York, 1952); in the two latter the matter is not even mentioned. The reasons for including the settlements among the earliest in the present study are shown in n. 17 below.

differences between the northern and southern groups are appreciable, but they are not great. The general level of the culture is about the same, a little better in the "Fayum-Merimde" group, but some particulars, of pottery and other things, are different. Both groups were of typically hoe-culture peoples. The pottery is crude, but by no means elementary. There were domestic cattle, sheep, and swine, but probably rather few, especially in the Fayum villages, and hunting game in the swamps was an important factor in livelihood. The grain raised was emmer wheat and barley.

The Fayum and Merimde sites were in regions where the desert was encroaching, if not at the moment when the settlements were made, then very soon afterwards.[12] The probability is that there was no year-round vegetation at either place and that no clearing of forest or draining of swamp had to be done. When the settlements were made, the Fayum Lake had probably no longer a direct water connection with the Nile[13] and so was not affected by the annual inundation, a notable advantage for primitives with little or no experience of water control. But this cannot have been the case at Merimde, and there are signs there of a pond, which may conceivably have been an elementary reservoir,[14] filled annually by the flood of the river. At Merimde, the settlement itself was on a small knoll, and it seems likely that the Rosetta branch flowed then where it does now, or somewhere quite near to the east. At Merimde some precautions must have been necessary at the time of the inundation, but we are without indication of what they were. In Upper Egypt, some, or all, of the Badarians, of their rather problematical prede-

[12] G. Caton-Thompson and E. W. Gardner, *The Desert Fayum*, I (London, 1934), p. 17 (Gardner), p. 89 (Caton-Thompson); H. Junker in *Anzeiger der Akademie der Wissenschaften in Wien*, 66 Jahrgang (1929), pp. 172-173.
[13] Caton-Thompson and Gardner, I, 88.
[14] Junker, p. 172.

cessors, the "Tasians,"[15] and of their successors, the "Am-ratians"—of whom more below—lived out of reach of the inundation on land dried or drying out below the scarp of the high desert. As to Frankfort's opinion that there were also peoples of this kind living on hillocks within the swampy belt, it remains a speculation.

In the last ten years opinion about the origin of all these early settlers has crystallized firmly: it is that they came from the south, Nubia or beyond. They were descendants of the people we met in the last chapter who left the western agricultural region long before the origin of civilized societies, and went by some route or other and established themselves in Abyssinia.[16] It is chiefly important to remember about them that the grains they brought to Egypt and at least one of the animals, their sheep, were of Asiatic, not of African, origin.

The Fayum settlements have been dated by the Carbon 14 method to between about 4500 and 4000 B.C.[17] I judge that

[15] The Tasians are often given as the earliest people in Upper Egypt, but they are a somewhat indefinite element in the record. They are frequently treated as a substantial and definite people, distinct from the Badarians, but their treatment by Brunton, their discoverer, hardly seems to warrant this; see G. Brunton, *Mostagedda and the Tasian Culture* (London, 1937). In Chapter II of this work (pp. 2-4), a catalog of the sites worked, it appears that at least sixteen Tasian villages were found, as well as many Tasian graves. But later (pp. 5, 8) Brunton confesses that it is extremely difficult to tell Tasian and Badarian remains apart, and in Chapter IV (pp. 7-25)—containing, according to its title, detail about Tasian and Badarian villages, but in its substance chiefly detail about graves—he frankly abandons the attempt to distinguish between the two types. In Chapter III (pp. 5-7) some forty Tasian burials are described so that my caution about acknowledging the distinct character of the Tasians may be thought excessively conservative, but even those burials Brunton admits are difficult to distinguish from Badarian ones. Cf. Baumgartel, pp. 20-21. Frankfort (*Birth of Civilization*, p. 41) avoids the necessity of distinguishing between Tasian, Badarian, and Amratian. (For the last, see text below.)

[16] Above, pp. 42-43.

[17] Willard F. Libby, *Radiocarbon Dating*, 2nd ed. (Chicago, 1955), pp. 77-78, items C-457, C-550, and C-551. The actual dates are, for C-457, 6054 ± 330 and 6136 ± 320, average 6095 ± 250 years ago, for C-550 and C-551, 6391 ± 180 years ago. The people in question are what Miss Caton-

they could have been earlier by a few centuries than 4500, however, for the grain taken from their granaries, on which the dating has been done, was, presumably, not the earliest grain the Fayumians raised. We have no Carbon 14 dates for the Badarians, but the Amratians (or "Nakada I" people), just mentioned above—who succeeded the Badarians, were much like them, and were certainly largely descended from them—have been dated by the Carbon 14 method to between 4000 and 3500 B.C.[18] It follows that the Badarians and Tasians were about contemporaneous with the Fayumians—a hypothesis which has long been in existence though it used to be thought that they were all some five centuries or more earlier than the carbon dates now suggest.

Yet another people, the "Gerzeans" (or "Nakada II" people), arrived in Egypt about 3000 B.C.[19] They came directly

Thompson calls the "Fayum A" people; the "Fayum B" people were not early settlers and are not considered in this book.

With every allowance made for the wide tolerances of radiocarbon dates, this is by far the earliest date we have for settlements in Egypt so that it becomes necessary to include the Fayum settlement among the earliest settlements there. This was the current opinion before Mrs. Baumgartel published *The Cultures of Prehistoric Egypt* in 1947, and we now, therefore, return to that opinion. The fact that the highest date indicated by the radiocarbon process may be as much as 500 years later—I do not think it could be more—than the original guess date Miss Caton-Thompson put forward is not really very startling. Mrs. Baumgartel's book remains an important contribution to Egyptian prehistory, but the specific practice of cross-dating on a basis of pottery, and still more of stone, types between places considerable distances apart, without outside confirmation in other terms, is now shown to be very rash.

[18] Libby, pp. 78-79, items C-810, C-811, and C-814, giving respectively 5744±300, 5619±280, 5577±300 years ago.

[19] Libby, p. 79, items C-812, 5020±290 years ago, and C-813, 4720±310 years ago. This date looks extremely near the traditional date of unification of Egypt, so that the Gerzean invasion and the unification *may* have been continuous events. But it is equally possible, on Carbon 14 evidence alone, that they were not, for the Gerzean invasion may have been as early as about 3300 B.C., and the unification may have been quite a lot later than 3000 B.C., viz. 2700, 2600, or even later; there are no Carbon 14 dates for Menes himself, and the ones there are for early pharaohs contradict one another hopelessly; see Libby, p. 77, items C-1, C-12 and C-267. For other considerations rendering discontinuity more likely, see n. 68 below.

from somewhere in southwest Asia within the western agricultural region, but we cannot tell from what part of the region.[20] This people, consequently, differed from the other early settlers in Egypt, all of whom came in the first instance from Africa, but the Gerzeans were by no means wholly without relationship to their predecessors and amalgamation proceeded.

In Chapter 1 it is mentioned that the first three types of settlers in Egypt showed no signs, visible to the archaeologist, of creating a civilized society. The people intended are the Fayumian-Merimdians, the Tasian-Badarians and the Amratians. There is no doubt that in the time of the Gerzeans the creation of the civilized society was begun—if it had not been begun before. It is quite clear in the archaeological record that the settlements beside the Fayum died out, or were abandoned;[21] the same is true of the one at Merimde. And there was little or no change, over the period of their existence, in the type of remains left respectively at the two places. As to the Tasian and Badarian remains, there was, no doubt, some change as between the two, but Brunton, their discoverer, says several times that it is extremely hard to tell them apart.[22] There was not much change between them, then, and such as there was quite possibly was the product of new immigration; there is no archaeological sign of the relatively rapid development characteristic of a civilized society. It is not so likely that the transition from Badarian to Amratian was due to new immigration, but after the transition there was again apparent stagnancy until the Gerzean invasion. In the archaeological records of these first three groups of peoples who settled in Egypt, then, we miss the only sort of sign we can use securely as evidence of civilized conditions.

[20] See Baumgartel, pp. 71-74; on p. 44, however, where the entry of this people into Egypt is discussed, there is hardly a remark with which I agree.
[21] Caton-Thompson and Gardner, I, 2.
[22] See n. 15 above.

But this is certainly no proof of a negative sign, and in any case, the evidence must also be considered in another way in our search for the origin of the Egyptian civilized society: even if the origin occurred only after the Gerzeans arrived, the descendants of the earlier peoples were certainly involved as well, for they were still present in Egypt, amalgamated with the Gerzeans, both in culture and in blood. It is not even justifiable to exclude the Fayumians, although their settlement beside the Fayum Lake was abandoned. Both the Fayumians and Merimdians probably moved to other places in the valley.

Mesopotamia has in the *Enuma Elish* the myth which most plainly, and indeed most artistically, describes the creation of the habitat of a valley society. We must be warned, however, that this myth, as we have it today, is a late redaction by learned priests who were eminently capable of improving upon earlier versions by direct observations from nature. The main valley had certainly been under the full control of man before their time, but they wrote in an age of transition, an age of decline in fact, when parts of the valley had been allowed to revert to their natural condition. Hence, there is some likelihood that the *Enuma Elish* was largely re-touched by new masters from the model.

The *Enuma Elish* postulates in the beginning a watery chaos, in which salt water, fresh water, and a third element which may be cloud or mist (the philologists have not yet quite identified it) were all mingled together; something like this condition often obtains now in the region where the Shatt-el-Arab and the Karun carry the waters of the Tigris and Euphrates into the Persian Gulf. After the commingling of the three waters, the emergence of the land began with the deposit of silt, consisting of a mixture of mud from the fresh water and salt from the salt water; such silt is in fact deposited now at the mouths of the Shatt-el-Arab and the Karun. Next came the formation of the horizon, of which there were both celestial and terrestrial elements; so may the horizon be seen from most points of observation within the valley of a river flowing through the desert. After this the sky and the earth were formed as two huge disks, each the product of one of the elements of the horizon. Finally, the two disks "were forced apart by the wind, who puffed them up into the great bag within which we live, its underside being the earth, its upper side the sky."[23]

The entire narrative so closely reflects the physical conditions of a valley in the desert before settlement by man that we may legitimately imagine assiduous priests—who, we know, were vigorously propagating a revised gospel in the early second millennium B.C., when the *Enuma Elish* was put together[24]—fitting the story carefully to the facts of nature in order the better to persuade the laity. We cannot be sure that the priests, as they worked on their cosmology, used material carried down from as far back as the actual time of settlement two thousand years earlier, but there is a reasonable probability that such materials had existed and, if they had, then that the *Enuma Elish* was ultimately derived from them, for, however much rewriting the priests did, they surely wanted to make use of the prestige of ancient scripture. All we actually know of the process of derivation, however, is some scraps of late intermediary versions of the myth.

The earliest settlers in Mesopotamia were those who established themselves in the lower part of the upper valley at Samarra and perhaps at Baghouz and other places,[25] but they

[23] Jacobsen in *The Intellectual Adventure of Ancient Man*, pp. 170-172.
[24] This was the time of decline of the Mesopotamian society at the end of the first cycle of its history when religion was being reconstructed; for cycles, see above, Ch. I, pp. 6-7.
[25] Braidwood not long ago permitted himself to "guess wildly" that the original settlement at Samarra near the Tigris and that at Baghouz on the

took no part in origination of the civilized society. Even these settlers, however, probably knew something about water-control,[26] for they had come from Iran, a country whose water supply was turbulent and hard to manage. But the civilized society arose in southern Mesopotamia. Excavation there has uncovered some of its first establishments. The earliest known was at Eridu (now Abu Shahrain), but those at the spot known now as al Ubaid and at Ur of the Chaldees are also original settlements, as are a number of later establishments. al Ubaid, Ur, and Eridu were all beside the Euphrates, which then ran west of its present course. The migrants had either crossed the valley territory from east to west in selecting their new places of settlement, or they had travelled by sea, coasting probably, across the Persian Gulf, for they too had come from Iran.[27]

Euphrates might have been the first fingering of settlers from the northern grass-lands towards the alluvium of the valley; *The Near East and the Foundations for Civilization*, p. 36, n. I see nothing horribly wild about this guess unless the term "northern grass-lands" contains some strange connotation. Wherever the grass-lands were, the settlers at Samarra surely got their pottery techniques from somewhere in the mountain fringe northward and eastward of Mesopotamia, or from further eastward in Iran, and the easiest deduction to make from this is that they themselves came from somewhere in that general region. Certainly, the settlers at Samarra are the earliest possible people we know of at present to settle in the Mesopotamian plain beside one of its main rivers.

[26] The remains at Samarra are graves, and they are located outside the valley depression up on the edge of the desert where the inundation cannot reach them. Herzfeld, their discoverer, makes the following remarks about them: "Spuren von Ansiedlung und etwa Wohnungen, kurz irgend etwas Anderes als Gräber, wurden nicht beobachtet. Daher ist es wahrscheinlich, dass die Menschen, denen die Gräber gehörten, wie die ackerbauenden Araber heutigen Tages, im Tigristale selbst wohnten, und dort auf den Inseln und an den Ufern des Stromes ihre Felder bestellten und ihre primitiven Ansiedlungen hatten, während sie ihre Toten auf dem hohen, überschwemmungsfreien Ufer bestatteten." (Ernst Herzfeld, *Die vorgeschichtlichen Töpfereien von Samarra, Die Ausgrabungen von Samarra*, V, Berlin, 1930, p. 1.) Cf. Frankfort's opinion about the earliest settlers in the Nile Valley; pp. 73 and 76 above.

[27] The correspondence between Iranian pottery and the early pottery at al Ubaid, Ur, and Eridu can be studied, with one exception, in D. E.

They may have come from the Iranian Plateau itself, where desiccation was advanced.[28] More probably, they came from the mountains of the western edge of the plateau,[29] where water courses down in the rainy season, making for a short time flood-beds which have to be rapidly and effectively used, the water thereafter becoming dangerously scarce for the rest of the year. In fact, experience with mountain floods may well have suggested the idea of moving to the alluvial plains of Mesopotamia if the people knew of them, which they probably did. Whatever their previous habitat was precisely— and some of them may have come from one kind of place, others from other kinds—these people knew a good deal about

McCown, *The Comparative Stratigraphy of Early Iran, Studies in Ancient Oriental Civilization*, no. 23 (Chicago, 1942), pp. 35-42. The exception is the earliest pottery at Eridu (which has been called "Eridu ware"; see Seton Lloyd and Fuad Safar, "Eridu," *Sumer*, IV [1948], 124-125), as to which I follow Frankfort, *Birth of Civilization*, p. 45, n. 1. The general relationships of the pottery can be amplified in Sir Aurel Stein, "An Archaeological Tour in the Ancient Persis," *Iraq*, III (1936), 111-230, and in Stein's *Old Routes of Western Iran* (London, 1940). On these two tours Stein shows that there was a large prehistoric population, of the kind which produced the pottery of the general Samarra-al Ubaid types, living in western Iran all the way from Fars up to Kurdistan; he shows too the main conditions in which that population lived.

[28] H. Bobek, "Klima und Landschaft Irans in vor- und frühgeschichtlichen Zeit," *Geographischer Jahresbericht aus Österreich*, XXV (1953-54), 22-23. Bobek gives minimum dates for desiccation as 9000-4000 B.C. It is clear that at least the second date should be a good deal later.

[29] Bobek's data are not taken from the western scarp of Iran, but from the Elburz to the north and from the plateau itself. The scarp is not waterless today, and I do not suppose that it was so in the fifth to fourth millennia B.C.; it must, in fact, have been one of those areas in which some rain continued to fall all through the period of desiccation. Stein reports extremely few signs of diminishment. Instead he constantly notices places which have today adequate water supplies and show signs of prehistoric establishments, and conversely of other places which have only artificial water supplies or none at all now, and have no signs either of inhabitation in prehistoric times; see "Tour in Persis," pp. 133, 153, 161, 182, 183; *Routes in Western Iran*, pp. 128, 220-221, 286. I do not think this means that there has been no diminishment of rain supplies since the fifth millennium, but merely that the reduction has not been large enough to be apparent without special geological study.

controlling the waters,[30] and in Mesopotamia they doubtless set about defending themselves from the river, as well as making use of it, as soon as they arrived.[31]

There are no Carbon 14 dates for any of the settlements in Mesopotamia with which we are concerned, but the northern settlement of Jarmo can be related in a rough way chronologically with the one at Samarra, and Jarmo is dated by the Carbon 14 method to the early centuries of the fifth millennium.[32] It is reasonable to guess, then, that Samarra belongs to the middle centuries of the fifth millennium, the beginnings at Eridu perhaps to a little later and at al Ubaid and Ur to about 4000 B.C.

The creation myths of Egypt and Mesopotamia, in the versions we have today, are compositions of societies in which the valley territory in the midst of desert still greatly preponderated in the high culture over all other territories which had been brought into the society. This is not the case with the Indian creation myth. The Indian creation myth survives in the *Rigveda*, in certain of the *Brahmanas* and in less important places. The *Brahmanas* are very late, sophisti-

---

[30] Stein finds their remains in mountains and upland territory near flood-beds and other sources of water, much of which must have required both careful conservation and strong diking; see n. 27 above. Near Firuzabad in Fars Stein found remains containing pottery of the al Ubaid type and a drain of burnt brick "obviously for carrying off rain-water." He remarks upon the early date of this interesting find and compares it with a similar one he found at Dabarkot in northern Baluchistan; "Tour in Persis," pp. 127-129. This illustrates the sort of experience the settlers in southern Mesopotamia had in water-control.

[31] I do not think Lees' and Falcon's findings about the geological character of southern Mesopotamia (see n. 1 this chapter) diminish the likelihood that the lower Euphrates in the Eridu-Ur region had all the qualities of a great river bordered with swamps and tough swamp vegetation. The probable conditions of settlement at Ur are in any case shown in Sir Leonard Woolley, *Ur Excavations*, IV, American Philosophical Society (Philadelphia, 1955), pp. 2-6 and Plates 72 and 83.

[32] Libby, pp. 79-80, items C-113, 6707 ± 320 years ago, and C-742, 6606±330 years ago.

cated compositions dedicated to high ecclesiastical purposes, and even the *Rigveda*, as we have it, is a late document much re-worked by priests.[33] By the time this sacred literature was composed the high culture of India was spreading far south-ward in the peninsula. Moreover, a great break had happened many centuries earlier when the society's center had shifted away from the valley of the Indus into the Ganges basin,[34] where the settlements were not in any wise confined to the actual valleys. Again, the Indo-European peoples who entered the society at that time and came to play a large part in its evolution had not had the experience of creating a civiliza-tion in a river valley or anywhere else; they had learned civili-zation from the descendants of those who had created it in the Indus valley. But the Indo-Europeans imported their own ideas of creation, which had nothing to do with river valleys, and these ideas went into the general fund of tradition the priests later drew upon for their cosmology.

There survives, nevertheless, in modern Indian myth an enormous quantity of matter concerned with water and at least suggestions that river water was once of great im-portance. The primordial waters figure largely as the source of all elements and things at the beginning of creation. It is, however, characteristic of the sophistication of Indian my-thology that creation and all other stages of development of the world occur repetitively in an unending series of cycles.

[33] For modern versions of the creation myth which have Vishnu as the creator, but retain some signs of an early river valley myth, see Heinrich Zimmer, *Myths and Symbols in Indian Art and Civilization*, ed. Joseph Campbell, Bollingen Series, No. VI (New York, 1946), pp. 51-53; D. A. Mackenzie, *Indian Myth and Legend* (London, n.d.), pp. 3-9. A very short, critical summing up of Indian creation myth occurs in P. Masson-Oursel, H. de Willman-Grabowska and P. Stern, *L'Inde antique et la civilisation indienne, L'évolution de l'humanité*, dirigée par Henri Berr, tome 26 (Paris, 1933), pp. 155-157; cf. K. W. Morgan, *The Religion of the Hindus* (New York, 1953), p. 87.

[34] Another cyclical transition like the one referred to above in Meso-potamia; cf. n. 24 above.

This certainly has nothing to do with origins in a river valley; neither do all manner of other embellishments which have intruded into the story. Even so, the primordial waters hold what was probably their original place.[35]

Direct archaeological knowledge of material origins in India is vastly inferior to the corresponding knowledge we have for Egypt and Mesopotamia. In the first place, the amount of exploration and excavation in the northern part of the territory of the Indian Society of the first cycle has been small and unsystematic, while in the southern territory, where much more exploration has been done, a special difficulty confronts the search for beginnings. The difficulty is the consequence of the rise of the river-plain, the river-bed, and the water-table by reason of the immense amount of silt brought down and distributed by the Indus during the many historic centuries when it has been uncontrolled. The present water-table is well above the original level of settlement at Mohenjo-daro and other southern sites, and the task of the excavator is thus rendered very difficult indeed.[36] No excavator has, in fact, reached bottom yet in any of the lower valley sites, and it will probably be a long time before any does.

Apart from these difficulties in the valley itself, there is another complication in the search for Indian beginnings—a complication which is, however, a matter of great intrinsic interest. This is the fact that in the belt of land between the western side of the lower Indus valley and the Kirthar Hills

[35] In one version of the Indian myth Brahman is said to have cast his seed into the waters, as Atum did in one version of the Egyptian myth (*The Intellectual Adventure of Ancient Man*, p. 54). This could be a common inheritance from primitive times, or it could be something picked up at a later time by one lot of theologians from the other. In neither case need this affect the authenticity of the primordial waters as a memory of settlement in a valley.

[36] See Sir Mortimer Wheeler, *The Cambridge History of India*, Supplementary Vol., *The Indus Civilization* (Cambridge, 1953), p. 26, for an attempt which was made to get down to virgin soil at Mohenjo-daro in 1950.

in Baluchistan and indeed far beyond the Kirthars westward a whole series of settlements, of apparently primitive farming villages, existed before at least the main *floruit* of the civilized society in its primary cycle. For all we know, primitive farmers may also have established themselves further north in unexplored land approaching the river there. Today the territory in Sind through which the Indus runs its lower course and the Baluchi territory west of it are very dry, approaching desert conditions (except actually in the valleys of the small tributaries of the Indus there), but it seems sure that it was far from this condition at the time the settlements were made. Various explanations of the change have been offered, but it seems most likely that two factors are involved in it, a change in the course of the Indian monsoon which may have watered the territory in the fourth and third millennia b.c., and the damage to the land itself usually done by primitive farmers, or, in a physiography like that of Sind, by almost any farmers.[37]

The search for physical origins in India, then, has hardly begun. Little can be done here, therefore, except to ask questions. Are the civilized people descended from the primitives of the Sind-Baluchistan area, or did they enter the river valley from a more northerly region? It can be argued, on two grounds, that they came from further north: the first is that

[37] Cf. Wheeler, pp. 4-8 and Stuart Piggott, *Prehistoric India*, Pelican Books (Harmondsworth, 1952), pp. 133-136. There is an alternative suggestion about the climatic change, to the effect that the change has been one in the route of the Atlantic rainstorms resulting from retreat of the ice in its last stages after the Würm III glaciation. The change in the incidence of the monsoon is, I think, more likely than this; there is too much mountain mass to the west of the Indus valley for rain from as far away as the Atlantic to get over. But the route of the monsoon winds might well be affected by the more constant force of the movement of atmosphere from the Atlantic (cf. above, Ch. 2, n. 4). Wheeler thinks (pp. 7-8) that damage by the farmers and other human influences were more important than actual diminution of rainfall. I agree, but I should like very much to know whether this means that the entire Thar Desert is man made; I suppose not.

86

the southern part of the territory has been fairly well explored by Sir Aurel Stein[38] and by Majumdar[39] without discovery of any clear trace of the ancestors of the civilized people;[40] the other is that, in the period of the civilized society which we know, the pottery has a red base color, and "red ware" is characteristic of northern Iran, while the Sind primitives derive from the "buff ware" province of southern Iran. This assumes, of course, that the civilized society began with red ware, which we do not know since we do not know its beginnings.

I do not believe, however, that the Indian Society started in the north, the Punjab territory through which the great tributaries of the Indus flow, and I doubt very much that Harrappā, the city on which that territory centers, was an early city.[41] I should suppose rather that the settlers struck the valley of the Indus itself first, as they would naturally do if they came from Iran in the west since the Indus flows farther west than its great tributaries do, and that they moved southward along the Indus, eventually developing the great

[38] *An Archaeological Tour in Waziristan and Northern Baluchistan*, Memoirs of the Archaeological Survey of India, no. 37 (Delhi, 1929); *An Archaeological Tour of Gedrosia*, Memoirs, no. 43 (Delhi, 1943), esp. pp. 7-13, 24-25.

[39] N. G. Majumdar, *Explorations in Sind*, Memoirs, no. 48 (Delhi, 1934).

[40] There are in the uplands and foothills of Baluchistan numerous dams and terraces, called locally *gabarband*, which testify to the catchment and storage of water there. There is no indication who built these so that it could be supposed that the ancestors of the civilized peoples did so. But I think it much more likely that such large and ambitious buildings were subsequent to the rise of civilization. See Stein, *Tour in Waziristan and Northern Baluchistan, passim.*

[41] Because the Harrappā type of remains appears fully developed overlying quite another type of remains in the citadel ("Mound AB") area (see Wheeler, p. 19 and section drawing opposite). Of course, developmental stages may be found in some other part of the remains of Harrappā, but, barring this, the meaning of the section seems to me to be that a large state which flourished at the climactic period of the civilization, expanded into the region of Harrappā from somewhere else (the south?) and there built this then new city.

center at Mohenjo-daro—though there could have been other earlier centers farther north on the main river.

If this is what happened, the "buff ware" settlements in Sind were taken in the rear, so to speak, by the settlers in the Indus valley. This seems rather probable since the typical styles of some of those settlements were, at a late stage in the careers of the settlements, influenced by the civilization, and began to produce pottery and other things showing that influence.[42] The spread of the civilized society over the region and especially along the coast northwestward into Makran is well shown, though it did not by any means swallow up all the primitives of the Sind-Baluchistan region, even all of a number of new settlers there who came in from Iran-Afghanistan to take advantage of trade, or of other sources of support which the presence of the civilized society afforded.

This is admittedly quite a speculative picture of the material origin of the Indian Society, but it accounts for the main

[42] At Amri on the Indus and at several other places "Amri" potsherds were found in a layer underlying a layer containing "Harrappā" potsherds. But the term "Harrappā," as applying to pot and all other types, means only the products of the civilization at its (apparently long enduring and long unchanged) climactic achievement. We have no record of it in formative phases, and it is quite possible that Amri culture is subsequent to, or contemporary with, formative phases of the civilized culture. Since it is the most prevalent apparently primitive culture on the west bank of the lower Indus, it could signify primitives establishing themselves in the land west of the valley after the civilized society had got started in the valley itself. It seems more likely that such a culture as Amri preceded the civilization. If so, it could prove that the Amri people participated in the civilization and even that their remains signify an early stage of it, including the stage of transition from primitive to civilized conditions. The Amri styles may well have endured in the more conservative regions of the society at a time when the advanced places, chiefly on the Indus itself, were producing quite different materials. The "Nal" pottery, which is related to Amri, looks like a later phase influenced by the leading Harrappā type. "Kulli" pottery, found in village remains chiefly in the Kolwa region beyond the Kirthars from the Indus plain, is another local product showing even stronger Harrappā influences. This resulted certainly from the extension of the high culture westward into Makran as the civilization grew.

facts known and runs counter to none of them, so far as I can judge. It has, even though speculative, a certain interest for present purposes because it implies that there was not a great deal of difference in the origin and early course of a primary civilized society established in a river valley, whether the river ran through desert or not, or whether, if not, the civilized society had primitive neighbors. We may add a further guess to those made already by supposing that Sind and Baluchistan, though not steppe and desert as they are now, were not very fertile and supported a somewhat small population. The life of that population seems to have been rather incidental to the life of the civilized society, whose chief directions of expansion were up-river and along the coast, probably southward to Cutch and Kathiawar as well as northwest to Makran.

We turn now to China. The Chinese Society, like the Indian Society, has long outgrown its original valley base, but the mythological evidence surviving is not, like that for the Indian Society, largely composed of modern survivals and records from times when the society had already moved away from its original valley. Almost all the evidence for the Chinese Society goes back to a time when the valley still predominated in its territory. That is an advantage.

But Chinese creation myths do not, like Egyptian, Mesopotamian, and Indian creation myths, begin with the primordial waters; nor do they describe very plainly a primeval valley before man came to settle in it. Instead, they concentrate upon formidable floods, episodes which occurred in the Mesopotamian and Indian societies only some considerable time after the earliest settlements, while Egypt either had no flood myth, or no such myth has come down to us. No mystery attends these differences. The flooding of North China in the early millennia of the final deglaciation was on a far greater scale than what happened at that time in the more westerly valleys.[43] There is, in fact, a significant contrast between North China and Indus India in this matter, for in North China the entire basin of the river system was heavily waterlogged and the country uninhabited, whereas in India, as we have seen, it is quite probable that primitives lived in the general region west of the river or rivers (though not of course in the great river valleys themselves), for many centuries before the civilized society began to be formed. The contrast cannot arise with Egypt and Mesopotamia, naturally, because there the rivers run through desert.

The Chinese flood-creation myths, therefore, record the experiences of the settlers who entered the country when the reduction of the excessive waters made it inhabitable. One myth records also the concomitant drying out of regions in the Gobi, which had been inhabitable when North China was not. Whether the myths record rather the settlement of primitives in North China or the foundation of the civilized society is scarcely a real question. As with Egypt, there is some doubt as to how soon the formation of the civilized society did begin, but there is no likelihood, as there is with India, that some neighboring primitives were unaffected by it. An opinion as to when and where the civilized society began to be formed and as to what peoples took part in it will be offered when all the evidence, mythological, archaeological, some of it geological, has been reviewed.

The myths fall into two lots. One lot, a pair, relates to flood control in Shansi and Honan. These are the myth of T'ai-t'ai and the most famous of all the myths, the myth of Yü. The other three, the myths of Niu-kua, Kung-kung and Ch'e-you, have been shown by Maspero to belong to the southwestern corner of Shantung.[44]

[43] See Ch. 2, p. 51.
[44] H. Maspero, "Légendes mythologiques dans le *Chou King*," *Journal Asiatique*, CCIV (1924), 1-100; *Mélanges posthumes sur les religions et*

The T'ai-t'ai myth recounts how T'ai-t'ai diked the River Fen, chief tributary of the Yellow River in Shansi, and the Fen's own tributary, the T'ao (now called the Su), and so drained the K'iu-yo basin, rendering the T'ai-yuan region inhabitable.[45] The Yü myth, among many other things, tells how Yü dredged a passage for the Yellow River itself, the defile of Meng-men, through the hills of Lung-men in northern Honan, and thereby saved "all China" from floods.[46]

The Niu-kua myth is a confused account of how Niu-kua dealt with a cosmic disorder in which the four cardinal points got out of place, the sky and the earth slipped out of their proper physical relation, fire burned continuously, and water overflowed. After righting these and other evils, Niu-kua created men out of yellow earth. The Kung-kung and Ch'e-you myths record the same cosmic disorder, but the Kung-kung myth ends, not with the creation of man, but with the rise of Hou-T'u, god of the soil. The Ch'e-you myth assigns the events to the time of the Yellow Emperor, who first, through various agents, had the earth inundated and then, being shown that this was a disaster, sent to earth Pa, goddess of desiccation. She was unable to return to heaven after she had done her work, and so was transported to the north, to the Gobi presumably, where she lives still.

The archaeological evidence shows first that simple farmers who had lived previously in Sinkiang and the Gobi entered all northern China from Kansu to Shantung and northeastern

<hr />

l'histoire de la Chine, I (Paris, 1950), 179-194; for centers of the various myths, *Journal Asiatique*, pp. 70-79; *Mélanges*, pp. 187-190. The myths are traced to their places of origin by survival today of cults of their heroes. Maspero follows the fashion of the time when he originally wrote this study in being extremely skeptical of the value of myths as sources for prehistory. This opinion I cannot accept.

[45] Maspero, in *Journal Asiatique*, CCIV, 51-52, 73-74; *Mélanges posthumes*, I, 190. The region contains an area still called T'ai-t'ai-chö (T'ai-t'ai's marsh) which, however, has long been dried out.

[46] Maspero in *Journal Asiatique*, CCIV, 48-51, 70-73; *Mélanges posthumes*, I, 189-190.

China as far as Jehol, probably farther.[47] These were the people who made a coarse grey pottery with comb and cord patterns and blobs on it. It shows next the establishment in Kansu of a people who made a painted pottery akin to that derived from Iran which was characteristic of all the earliest settlers in Mesopotamia and of the Gerzean settlers in Egypt.[48] This pottery spread from Kansu into Shensi, Shansi and Honan, but it did not last long in this extension (whereas it did in Kansu), and opinion mostly is that few, if any, of the Kansu people themselves moved eastward.

The Kansu establishment must have been of acutal migrants from the west, and these were not the only ones from the west: quite soon there came also a people who made a fine black pottery. They have been called the "Lungshan" people in their Chinese establishments, and Heine-Geldern has called them the "East Caspian" people in one of their important establishments further west.[49] Heine-Geldern thinks they came ultimately from Eastern Anatolia, and, certainly, they or their cultural relatives are well-known in many western Asiatic and southeastern European places. The Lungshan people did not enter China through Kansu, perhaps because they found painted pottery people already in possession there.[50] They moved north, but did not descend directly upon Shensi or Shansi either—again because strong peoples were in possession there. They entered North China proper by Shantung, eastern Honan, and Anhwei, afterwards pene-

[47] See Max Loehr, "Zur Ur- und Vorgeschichte Chinas," *Saeculum*, III (1952), 15-31, for those peoples and their variations and cultural descent; p. 32 contains a table showing where their pottery and other pottery have been found in North China.

[48] Loehr, pp. 33 ff.

[49] R. Heine-Geldern, "China, die ostkaspische Kultur und die Herkunft der Schrift," *Paideuma*, IV (1950), 53-60 = *Mythe, Mensch und Umwelt*, ed. A. E. Jensen (1950), pp. 53-60.

[50] Sidney Kaplan, "Early Pottery from the Liang Chu Site, Chekiang Province," *Archives of the Chinese Art Society of America*, III (1948-1949), 39-40.

trating *westward* into western Honan and still later south-westward as far as Szechuan.

The T'ai-t'ai myth is simple and rational and may well be thought to recall the experiences of very early settlers, presumably coarse pottery people, in Shansi. The Yü myth is far more complex, containing a variety of marvels, and a part of it is political, Yü being described as the founder of the "Hsia Dynasty." That event, if event it was, probably occurred after the contact of the settlers in the Honan-Shansi region with the painted pottery tradition. It is of some interest that a son of Yü, Hsia-hou Ch'i, is said to have lived still in the Gobi[51] so that the remaining oases in the desert may well have continued to form a part of the culture area after the establishment of migrants in North China had taken place.

However old some elements in the three Shantung myths are, it is not unreasonable to associate them in part with the Lungshan people, for Shantung was a key territory in their entry into China. It is also of importance that southwestern Shantung is very near the last bend the Yellow River takes in its course to the sea. The vicinity of that bend long remained, indeed remains still, one of the most dangerous places near the river. The river constantly breaks its banks there, and has often changed its course, reaching the sea at points far distant from one another and flooding huge areas of populated land on the way. It is no wonder then, that southeastern Shantung produced flood myths. It is interesting that one of those myths contains the lethal heat goddess Pa, and that the composers of the myth thought that Pa had been sent down to earth to remedy the floods. That reverses the order in which human beings had encountered the two scourges, but it is not a bad interpretation of the cosmic process it seeks to explain.

[51] Loehr, p. 52.

There is one matter on which at present there is no archaeological evidence, the entry of peoples from the south, the
Yangtze valley and beyond, into North China, as North
China became inhabitable. But some of the myths, in my
opinion, strongly suggest that this happened, for, as Maspero
has shown, there are certain parallels between the North
Chinese myths and those of the Lolo of South China and of
the white Tai of Phu-qui, Indochina.[52] We cannot tell from
this evidence, however, when the southern peoples began to
move into North China and whether or not they were involved in the origin of the civilized society there.

Owen Lattimore gives the opinion that Chinese civilization
originated on the tributaries of the Yellow River in the loess
hills of northwestern China[53]—that is to say, in Shansi,
Shensi perhaps, and western Honan. All the evidence, I
think, points to that region and not to Shantung and eastern
Honan, where a rival opinion places it.

The northwestern hill country is geologically of a special
character. The quantities of loess covering it are the greatest
in the world, in many places hundreds of feet deep. The loess
was blown as very fine dust swept up by the wind off frozen,
but not snow or ice-covered, ground in the far northwest

[52] *Journal Asiatique*, ccɪv, 60-70; *Mélanges posthumes*, I. This is, I
believe, the real meaning of the resemblances of the Chinese to the southern
legends, viz. that some of the southern ideas were brought into the Chinese
conglomerate myth, and not, as Maspero thinks, that they were all of a
common origin, and certainly not that none of them had more than a sort
of fortuitous application to particular places.

[53] *Inner Asian Frontiers of China*, American Geographical Society Research Series, no. 21 (London and New York, 1940), pp. 29-32, 261-262.
Lattimore considers the beginning of agriculture in China to be a part of
the origin of Chinese civilization, and his view that the origin was in the
loess country subsists chiefly in the idea that it was easy for a hunting
and gathering people to make the transition there. No such transition
was, in fact, made there. Nevertheless, the loess country would have been
a good region for agriculture to get established in, and, by the same token,
it *was* a good region for primitive farmers to make permanent settlements
in. And that certainly led up to the origin of civilization.

94

during the Quaternary glaciations, and deposited on the hills of Kansu, Shensi, Shansi and Honan which slowed up the wind. During the main periods of deposit of the loess the Yellow River did not exist; its waters were frozen at their sources in Tibet. Probably the loess country itself was frozen too so that there were no small rivers of local origin either. In each interglacial, however, these conditions ceased; though some loess was still blown in, it was much less, and the waters emerged again. Whether in every interglacial an initial water-logging of the country was followed by slow drying out and a return of aridity, we need not inquire. That, however, has been the course of events since the Würm III maximum, as we have already noticed in Chapter 2. Thus, there came a time, in the fourth or early third millennium B.C., when the land became inhabitable and particularly advantageous to agricultural peoples. The advantage lies chiefly in the excellent quality of the loess soil, which is almost as fertile as water-laid alluvium, having within it the decayed vegetation of surfaces constantly being covered with new aeolian deposits of soil. There were no great forests to clear, but rather grass and scrub, and the soil is very easily worked.

It was to this country that all the primitives gravitated. First came those from near at hand northward, the makers of coarse, grey, comb-marked, pottery. Then, since desiccation was still in progress in the western desert belt as well as the eastern, painted pottery people came and established themselves in Kansu. Finally, the Lungshan people, also from the west, who had circled about the loess country northward, approached it from the east, together with such of the local primitives of the north and east as had joined them in their movement. These various peoples began by settling beside the tributaries of the Yellow River, for the tributaries at that time ran across the surface of the loess, or quite near the surface, whereas the main river, bringing huge quantities of water down from the high mountains, had already cut its way down through the loose, friable loess until it flowed through much of the territory at the bottom of a gorge.

It is not sure how long settlement beside the tributaries met the needs of the settlers, but probably only for several centuries. The rain supply of the territory has always in postglacial times been very variable from year to year and only in rare good years enough to water crops directly and/or to replenish surface water supplies. It follows that the heavy annual melts of declining glaciation were what rendered the country for a time so attractive, and those must naturally have decreased as time passed. Further, as Andersson has shown, over a period of time the small streams have followed the history of the main river by cutting down their beds through the loess.[54] The water level has, in fact, fallen about 120 feet between the time of settlement and now. It must be supposed that sinking of the water level led the villagers first into the valley of the Yellow River in the loess uplands— something which was already happening when the Yü myth was composed. But no considerable population could be accommodated at the bottom of the gorge, or on its sides where the cliffs flanking it are less than sheer. People displaced by the drop in the water level and excess population resulting from the society's natural increase must, therefore, eventually have been compelled to pass on down river beyond the uplands into the open plain.

Thus, the environmental aspect of the origin of the Chinese Society is a matter of very special interest. The analogy of the loessic soil with an alluvial soil suggests that in the loess-covered uplands the settlers might have attained both the permanence and the closeness of settlement which other settlers did in the valleys of the great rivers of the Middle and

[54] J. G. Andersson, *Children of the Yellow Earth: Studies in Prehistoric China* (New York, 1934), pp. 156-187.

96

Near East. Yet there was actual permanence, in all likelihood, only for those who found space at the bottom of the gorges of the Yellow River and its tributaries and, to some extent, on the sides of the gorges.

Where and when, then, did the civilized society begin to be formed? I think it probably began beside the tributaries in the hills, but continued in the main valley, both as it passed through the loess country and after it reached the North China Plain to the east of the loess country. It cannot be said that the archaeological remains show the rapid development characteristic of civilized societies. Occasionally they do, for example at Hsi-yin-ts'un and neighboring large sites in southern Shansi.[55] But no general succession of changes concerning any large part of the region can yet be reliably constructed.[56] I think this is not more than deficiency of the presently known record, together with confusion caused by the rather frequent arrival of new peoples in many of the sites and consequent changes in the record brought about otherwise than by development. It cannot be said positively that the very simple peoples from the Gobi and beyond began the creation of the civilized society before others joined them.

It is nevertheless sure that these earliest peoples and the later ones too were all refugees from desiccation before they arrived in their new homes and that most of them met the same peril again in later periods in the loess country. The myths show that they encountered the danger of floods in the loess country, and there can be no doubt at all that those of them who later moved eastward into the plain met the same danger. They probably had, therefore, a somewhat checkered career—which is certainly not unusual for those who originated the primary civilized societies. The settlers in Meso-

[55] See Loehr, pp. 41-43.

[56] Only rather broad ones, not covering details or all sites found, are useful; for two of these, see chronologies cited in next note.

potamia surely had it as well, and, if we happened to know enough about the sojourn of those settlers in the hills of the Iranian scarp, we might feel it necessary to include that region, or a part of it, in the original base of the Mesopotamian Society. At any rate, there can be no reasonable doubt that the loess uplands of North China were part of the original base of the Chinese Society, or that they remained ever afterwards within the society's territory.

Rough dates, not based upon the Carbon 14 process, are all that can be offered. I think the earliest settlements, those of the migrants from the Gobi and Sinkiang, were about 2500 B.C. or perhaps a little earlier. The painted pottery influence— and people?—were in Shansi before 2000 and the Lungshan people a century or two later. The movement eastward onto the North China Plain could have begun at any time between 1850 and 1650.[57]

The last among the primary civilized societies to arise in a river valley was the Andean Society. This society arose in the valleys of some of the numerous short rivers which cross the coastal plain of modern Peru from the Andes to the Pacific Ocean. Here, again, is the familiar physiography of desert and river valleys, but it is quite special and different from the physiography of the valley societies of the Old World in that the rivers are numerous, short so far as their passage across desert goes, and that their passage was transverse through the territory of the society instead of longitudinal; that the desert itself is ribbon-shaped, running between mountains and coast; and that very high mountains flank the desert on the one side and the ocean flanks it on the other. There are some upland valleys and other intermount areas between the high sierras and the outer, lower mountain chains and spurs nearer

[57] Loehr (p. 51) gives a chronology; cf. C.F.A. Schaeffer, *Stratigraphie comparée et chronologie de l'Asie Occidentale (IIIe et IIe millénaires)*, (Oxford, 1948), p. 604.

the coast. These upland territories may have been, but probably were not, part of the civilized society's site at the time of its origin. All of them were drawn into its territory in later days. Thus the site of the society is dissimilar as well as similar to the sites of the Old World valley societies. Whether the Andean Society consequently developed special characters, different from some of the characters of the Old World societies, we cannot clearly discern; on the whole, however, it was much more like those societies than unlike them. In fact, reason will appear in Chapter 5 for thinking that in one rather special respect the Egyptian Society was the one different society and not the Andean Society.

Knowledge of creation, or origin, myths for the Andean Society is poor. This is for the reason that it has come to us after the utter ruin of the society by the Spanish conquerors and, for the most part, through the agency of Spanish clergy, who were indeed much interested in the mythology of the Andean peoples, but apt to compare and confound it with Christian mythology, most of which they still believed to be historical fact.[58] A flood, or floods, figure largely in the Andean myths. The flood myths certainly commemorate disasters brought about in early times by earthquakes, landslides, etc., for these seismic movements undoubtedly occurred then, as they still do today.[59] The myths also in all likelihood recall disasters resulting from the great rainstorms which fall upon the entire territory, coastal plain and mountains to-

[58] See the collections of Christoval de Molina and Francisco de Avila in *Narratives of the Rites and Laws of the Yncas,* ed. and trans. Clements R. Markham, Hakluyt Society (London, 1873), pp. 4-15, 132-144; cf. P. A. Means, *Ancient Civilizations of the Andes,* 2nd ed. (New York and London, 1936), pp. 52, 423.

[59] These remarks do not mean that I credit the opinions of Julio Tello and Rebeca Carrión Cachot about the destruction of the society of the Chavín period by a general seismic disaster; see Carrión, *La cultura Chavín,* Revista del Museo Nacional de Antropología y Arqueología, II, no. 1 (Lima, 1948), pp. 169-172.

gether, at intervals of years, sometimes as much as twenty years. The latter climatic spasms proceed from occasional displacement of the usual Pacific wind currents, and, except on those occasions, there is virtually no rainfall in the coastal plain where the Andean Society arose.

The Andean flood myths would not be of interest here if it were not for the fact that, like the Chinese flood myths, they have become involved with creation myths. They differ from most of the Chinese myths, however, in that much of the creation, even the creation of the heavenly bodies, seems to have occurred after the flood. The Andean peoples—as related by their Spanish interlocutors—identified themselves with the peoples who came after the flood and were a part of the creation then undertaken by the Supreme Being; the peoples who lived before the flood and were overwhelmed by it they considered alien. These notions may possibly mean that the Andean peoples who built up the civilization entered the society's territory at some time after a great flood had taken place, but there is at least one reason for rejecting that idea. It is that the myths do not tell anything about physiography, such as Egyptian and Mesopotamian creation myths do; the Andean myths might also be expected to do so if they really related to the early days of settlement, when the settlers were newly concerned with the physiography of their environment.

By contrast with the myths, archaeology is today beginning to outline a story about the settlement which may eventually be as clear as the stories about Egypt and Mesopotamia. There are, of course, some novelties in the Andean story. Thus, we meet in the earliest Andean settlements a class of cultivators whose counterparts in the Old World we should much like to meet, but have not yet done so. These people have been mentioned already both in Chapter 1 and Chapter 2. They made no pottery, and they knew no cereal; their cultivation of food included only squash, certain peppers and

100

beans (*canavalia*). Other vegetable food they probably gathered wild. They had no domestic animals and they were not even hunters. They were great eaters of shellfish, and they also caught vertebrate fish and sea-lions.[60] These people, of the "Cerro Prieto" culture, seem not to have been valley-dwellers at all; they lived beside the seashore, and their livelihood came chiefly from the sea.[61] They are best known from the seashore on the northern coast of Peru near the mouths of the rivers Chicama and Virú, but they probably lived also at many other points on the coast of Peru and possibly further south.[62] Two sites, which may have Cerro Prieto remains, have been found right in the Virú valley, close to the river itself. At the moment it is not possible to determine whether the earliest remains at the two sites really do indicate human occupation at all, but it looks as if they do. If so, these simple people made some sort of use of the river, or of its products.

We have a Carbon 14 date for the earliest settlers just out-

[60] Junius B. Bird, "Preceramic Cultures in Chicama and Virú," *A Reappraisal of Peruvian Archaeology*, Memoirs of the Society for American Archaeology, no. 4 (Menasha, 1948), pp. 21-28.

[61] Gordon R. Willey, *Prehistoric Settlement Patterns in the Virú Valley, Perú*, Smithsonian Institution, Bureau of American Ethnology, Bulletin 155 (Washington, 1953), pp. 38-40, 42.

[62] There is a mound similar to those near the mouths of the Chicama and the Virú at Aspero, Puerto de Supe, and there are other sites at Pachacamac and Chilca (Willey, *Prehistoric Settlement Patterns*, p. 400; W. D. Strong, G. H. Willey, and J. M. Corbett, *Columbia Studies in Archaeology and Ethnology*, I, no. 1, New York, 1943, pp. 12, 18-19). A considerable number of apparently similar remains have recently been found on the southern coast of Peru between the mouths of the rivers Nazca and Lomas (W. D. Strong, "Recent Archaeological Discoveries in South Central Peru," *Transactions of the New York Academy of Sciences*, series 2, XVI [1954], 216). The latter materials still need verification, and it is usual to consider more developed remains on the southern part of the coast to be later than corresponding ones on the northern coast. That, however, is no reason why the same should be true of the earliest types. For the moment, it is my guess that all these very early type remains, from north to south, are about contemporaneous.

side the Chicama valley: it is between 2500 and 2000 B.C.[63] The culture lasted there unchanged until something like 1300 B.C.,[64] when a certain enlargement began, the most notable element of which was the addition of crude pottery. It is possible that a new people came in, bringing with them these innovations, but, if the sites of their occupation are a guide, they were few. These are the people of the "Early Guañape" period. They too may have had stations of some sort within the valley. Some centuries later maize and a few other novelties appeared. The change is found on the rivers Chicama and Virú about 1000 B.C., or rather earlier, with the "Formative Cupisnique" and "Later Guañape" remains with which a new era in the origin of the society began, for it was then that the settlers established themselves securely in the valleys of the rivers and became river valley people in the true sense.

All the Guañape and Cupisnique remains, including Pre-Cupisnique or Formative Cupisnique, belong to the category general for the Andean Society, called "Chavinoid," after the place, Chavín de Huántar, where the general type was first found. Chavinoid materials are without doubt the product of the earliest long sustained period of the civilization; they must include, I believe, the first actually civilized remains, and their character will be shown in Chapter 5 to be very important for early religion. But the actual beginnings of the Chavinoid period of the civilization are not yet known. It has been shown by Strong and Evans that the earliest Chavinoid remains yet known are those in the Chicama, Santa Catalina, and Virú valleys,[65] the remains which have

[63] Libby, pp. 132-133, items, C-313, C-316 and C-598, giving 4257 ± 250, 4380 ± 270, and 4298 ± 230 years ago respectively.

[64] Libby, p. 133, item C-75, 2665 ± 200 years ago; J. L. Kulp, "Lamont Natural Radiocarbon Measurements, II," *Science*, CVI (1952), 412, no. 122A, 3149 ± 90 years ago.

[65] W. D. Strong and C. Evans, Jr., *Cultural Stratigraphy in the Virú Valley, Northern Peru: The Formative and Florescent Periods* (New York, 1952), pp. 229-237.

just been discussed above, but it has also been shown, not perhaps quite so decisively, by the same scholars that those are not the actual beginnings of the style.[66]

It has rather been implied here so far that the civilized society, and hence the Chavinoid style or styles, originated in some of the coastal valleys in the Chicama-Virú region, and I think it probable that they did so. There is, however, a rival theory which must have brief attention for two reasons; this is the theory of Julio Tello and his followers.[67] The reasons are that it contains certain intrinsic merits and that it at least suggests the direction from which the originators of the civilized society came. The theory—so far as it need be considered here—is that in its earliest beginnings the Chavinoid culture appeared on the eastern slopes of the Andes in the Huallaga region, and thereafter moved on first to the Western Andes and then to the coast. But these "beginnings" were really primitive culture traits. It could prove that some of the ancestors of the earliest civilized people, but not the civilized people themselves, lived in the Huallaga region, the traits brought from there being simply inheritances from primitive times, such as are found in all civilized societies in their early days.

Actually, it may be thought that an upland origin for the society could better be sought in the intermount regions mentioned above, west of the high sierra. There must have been many regions adjacent to the desert patches, from the great Sechura Desert in the north on southward, which had long been drying out at the time of origin of the civilized society. Demographic conditions were no longer as they had been two thousand years earlier when agriculture first appeared in the western South American region; there had been a

[66] Strong and Evans, p. 237.

[67] Julio C. Tello, *Origen y desarrollo de las civilizaciones prehistoricas Andinas* (Lima, 1942), pp. 69-93, 122-124; Carrión, *passim*.

great tightening up under the agricultural regime. Primitive farmers living anywhere on the expanding fringes of the desert areas in the late second millennium B.C. were probably compelled by population pressure elsewhere to seek refuge either in an upland valley, or in any of the coastal valleys— or first in an upland valley, which would have been the easier for them, and then in a coastal valley with more violent inundations and stronger swamp vegetation. If, indeed, they did resort first to one and then to the other, there is a parallel with the proto-Chinese who first settled in the loess hills of northwest China and with the proto-Mesopotamians who, previous to their settlement on the Euphrates, lived in the mountain edge of the Iranian Plateau. And, if something of this sort happened, I should expect it will be difficult, and rather unimportant, to discover how much of the emergence of the civilized society occurred in the first and how much in the second kind of environment. In any case, it is no use hoping to get anywhere with such a question until far more archaeological search has been made in the upland regions than the very meager amount which has been made there until now.

A few general observations may close this survey of the early lodgment of human population in the sites of the valley civilized societies.

The map of the desert belt of the northern hemisphere of the Old World, never to be simply interpreted, is somewhat deceptive as a guide to the origin of the valley societies. Every one of the rivers involved passes today through desert, but we have good reason to think that the Indus did not do so at the time of origin of the Indian Society. Moreover, it has never been suggested that the Chinese Society arose on that stretch of the Yellow River which passes through desert, the great northern loop through the Gobi and around the Ordos. Proximity of rivers to desert is not, as we can now plainly see, a sign of a simple conjunction of cause: the old idea that peoples living in the land which became desert moved out of that land as it did so and took refuge directly in the valleys is gone forever. Instead, the wide stretch of desert is to be taken only as a general indication, though a very telling one, that shortage of water supply was the dominating factor in human fortunes throughout the territory; the flight of humanity from the true desert country had taken place several, perhaps many, millennia before the civilized societies arose; and, the peoples who came to settle in the river valleys came, not from regions which were most desiccated, but from those which were least desiccated, in the general desert belt.

Next, we have, as forecast at the beginning of the chapter, found an element of gradualness in the approach made by most of the settlers to the river valleys. We know nothing, unfortunately, about India in this respect. China, however, offers the classic case of farming peoples who lived first on tributaries of the great river and there learned something about how to manage river waters, and then moved toward the river itself where it was certainly turbulent, but in most places could not cause floods because it was shut within a gorge. Even so, the settlers learned some more about managing the main river on an exceptional stretch where it could and did overflow, as is shown plainly in the Yü myth: the Yü myth is quite explicit that they learned to dredge rather than to depend on diking alone. After that, the Chinese moved on to tackle the Yellow River in the open plain, where it was probably the most dangerous of all the rivers the primary civilized peoples encountered. The approach of the proto-Chinese, or the very early Chinese, to the site of their civilized society was gradual in the special sense that physiography

105

itself took charge, so to speak, and led them in three steps to establish themselves in the valley.

By contrast, the first three groups of settlers in Egypt seem to have got stuck for a long time at the far outside edge of the valley beyond reach of the inundation. It is true that, according to Frankfort, there were establishments of these peoples right in the valley on hillocks sticking up above the swamps, but I think that, if this was so at all, those establishments were probably not more than outposts, hunting lodges perhaps, or possibly points at which it was safe to get water. There is some tentative evidence of similar establishments right in the valley swamp of one of the Andean rivers, and the first people who used those were the coastal fishing people who cannot be considered civilized in any sense applicable in this study. It is to be remembered that both in the Nile valley and on the Andean coast there is virtually no rain, and any people who contrived to survive there had to have access to the river water since there was no other water.

When the earliest proto-Andeans (the Early Guañape people) did appear, the gradual approach to the river valley began, but we know very little yet about it. With the arrival of the fourth of the proto-Egyptian peoples (the Gerzeans) the approach must have begun in Egypt as well. In the Egyptian case, and even perhaps in the Andean case, it is safe to see the beginnings of the approach in what the earlier peoples knew about the river and the use of its waters. And I think the increase in numbers of people, gradual in the Andean case, quite sudden in the Egyptian case, enforced bolder courses for sheer need of space; in fact, the old combination of forces, in its operative form of pressure of numbers upon land resources, gave a last push in both cases.

The case of Mesopotamia looks different, but is really much the same as the others. The gradualness appears to be missing since there was a definite break in the succession of events when the proto-Mesopotamians arrived from Iran and settled beside the lower Euphrates. If indeed we disregard what happened before the settlers arrived in the close vicinity of the river, we may say that the settlement in Mesopotamia was quite different from the other settlements in that the settlers arrived from some hundreds of miles away and could immediately settle beside the great river, applying there at once water control methods the settlers in other valleys had to learn painfully and perilously after they arrived in the new habitat. The argument proceeds that the proto-Mesopotamians had learned their technique of water control in their old habitat (Iran), something which none of the other settlers had done. Hence, the case of Mesopotamia is the exception which proves the rule that the settlers who began the creation of the primary civilized societies in river valleys could not cope with the waters when they first arrived, but had to serve a preliminary period on the outskirts of the valley, or somewhere not very far away, while they learned the arts of water control.

But "rules" of this sort are not much more than subjectivistic devices of scholarship, not perhaps wholly without value as theoretical instruments, but with little substance. The proto-Mesopotamians were really not different from all the other creators of valley societies, for they too had to learn the arts of water control. Nor is Iran, where they learned them, any further away from the lower Euphrates than the upper tributaries of the Yellow River, where the proto-Chinese learned similar arts, are from the main lower course of the river across the North China plain. The contrast is rather between the closeness to the main site of the society in the Egyptian and Andean cases, and the moderate distance— I estimate it at between 200 and 300 miles—in the Mesopotamian and Chinese cases. That contrast is quite a minor matter, a mere rider on the main thesis.[68]

The water control which all these people learned, in one place or another, sooner or later, was of the greatest practical importance among the early steps in the formation of the valley primary societies. But it must be understood as limited in scope. It is hardly to be described as irrigation in the sense of conducting water to otherwise dry fields which could not have been used without it. Irrigation in that sense was indeed developed on a great scale in all the valley societies of which we know something (in all, that is, except India, where it surely must have happened too at some time). But the development came much later; it came in response to a new problem of numbers which arose when the societies were in the heyday of the first cycles of their history; and that is another story, not treated in this book. The early water control in the valley societies was probably chiefly diking and dredging for protection against the inundation. The inundation itself was the chief irrigator, and, if in some of the societies there was a little more, some of which *would* come under the dictionary definition of irrigation, it was marginal to flood control.

Finally, we come to the climates of the river valley societies. All except one of the societies were in sub-tropical country. The one exception is China; that had a temperate climate. The climate of the Andean Society—though the society was nearer to the equator than the other four—was probably

[68] The theory of peculiarity of the Mesopotamian case can be impugned also in another way: the Gerzeans, who came from the same general primitive culture province as the proto-Mesopotamians did, may, like the latter, have brought a knowledge of water control with them and have set to work to apply it in Egypt as soon as they got there. Actually, I do not think they did this; there are a number of their early settlements, both in the direction of the Fayum and in the Wadi Hammamat, which suggest preliminary settlement before settlement in the inner valley. A case against that can be made by special pleading even so.

cooler than that of the other three in the sub-tropical zone. It stands to reason that differences of rain supply, an element in climate, cannot have been very important to societies whose water was essentially that taken from their respective rivers. But the rain supplies did, in fact, vary from none or very little in Peru and Egypt, to occasional torrents each year in Mesopotamia and China and worse torrents in Peru at intervals of up to twenty years, to normal monsoon rains for most years in India.

It is not yet evident that climate as a total factor was unimportant in the origin and growth of the valley societies. On that subject it is advisable to suspend judgment until the end of the next chapter where there will be a good many more data about climate, not only of the valley societies, but of all the primary civilized societies considered together.

MIDDLE AMERICA AND CRETE

Two of the seven primary civilized societies oirginated, in all likelihood, in country entirely different from river valleys. The Cretan Society originated in an island, rather a small one, and the Middle American Society in a broad territory, much of which was tropical forest.

The Cretan Society came to cover the center and the east of the island of Crete and expanded to some of the Cyclades Islands and to the Peloponnese, which was much later to become a part of European Greece. The Middle American Society came to cover a large tract of various country, running from Vera Cruz and the Valley of Mexico in the northwest, and from the Yucatan Peninsula in the northeast, to Guatemala and part of Honduras in the south.

It may seem strange that so special a process as the rise of a civilized society out of primitive conditions could take place elsewhere than in a river valley since river valleys are very special physiographically, and their special physiography undoubtedly fits intimately into the special process of rise of civilized societies. In view of these considerations, it must be said at once that there is a marginal possibility that the Middle American Society did actually start its career in a valley—but that even if it did, it very early expanded beyond its valley and spread into quite different country. It cannot reasonably be suggested that the Cretan Society began in a valley, but it is not impossible that a small river in the island was, for a very short time, of special use to the settlers there. The trouble is that we have no quite decisive data on absolute origins for either society. Even so, there are good reasons for supposing that the broader environments in which we know the two societies soon after their origin could have served, by different means in the two instances, as the special environments of origin of civilized societies. These means will, of course, be explained below.

The same three factors drove people to establish themselves in Crete and Middle America as in the five valley territories: desiccation, numerical increase, and wastage of soil. In the case of the Middle American Society there is no mystery as to where, and not much as to how, the three factors operated. In the case of the Cretan Society, it needs to be explained how the peoples involved came to the island, but that poses no great problem either.

The sources of information for the origin of these societies are, again, the same as for the valley societies: archaeological data together with a few literary data of later times which throw light backward in time, geologic-physiographic data, and myths.

The broad territories of the Middle American Society at an early time covered the lowlands at the base of the Yucatan Peninsula and in coastal Vera Cruz, with the uplands of Chiapas in between, and a little other low-lying country farther south in Honduras. They covered besides an amount of highland country in Guatemala and Oaxaca and had an extremely important highland development in the Valley of Mexico. The lowlands were tropical rain forest; the highlands entirely different country, with a more or less temperate climate. In the Valley of Mexico a climate which veered over rather long periods of time (on a historical-social scale) between wet and dry obtained.[1] About the time of the origin of the civilized society the climate there was still wet, but probably already declining into a long dry phase.

There is no possibility that the civilized society originated in the Guatemala or Oaxaca highlands. Oaxaca was somewhat behind all other regions of the society except the Guatemala highlands, and the Guatemala highlands were, clearly, provincial territory, following the adjacent lowland territory of central Yucatan in development and never, so far as archaeology shows, participating in the highest attainments of the civilization at all. The question where the civilized society actually took its rise is between the Valley of Mexico and the general lowland region—not, in my opinion, only the lowlands of central Yucatan, but the lowlands all taken together.

Again in my opinion, none of the earliest archaeological finds known at present could be of the actual origin of the society; they are all somewhat later.[2] But they are not much later, and it is not unlikely that they point the way toward the place where the origin was. As to whether the forest materials or those of the Valley of Mexico are earlier, I am strongly influenced by the argument of MacNeish.[3] He considers that the earliest materials found in the Huasteca region, in southern Vera Cruz, in central Yucatan and the Petén and in the Yojoa region of Honduras, all four of these lowland territories, were earlier than the earliest materials that have been found in the Valley of Mexico or in any other of the highland

---

[1] Paul B. Sears, "Pollen Profiles and Cultural Horizons in the Basin of Mexico," *The Civilization of Ancient America: Selected Papers of the XXIXth International Congress of Americanists*, ed. Sol Tax (Chicago, 1951), pp. 57-61.

[2] For reasons for this opinion, see text below, next paragraph.

[3] R. S. MacNeish, *An Early Archaeological Site Near Panuco, Vera Cruz*, Transactions of the American Philosophical Society, no. XLIV, Part 5 (Philadelphia, 1954), pp. 619-624.

regions. This opinion is based purely on relative types of pottery and other artifacts in the various places, and it could be proved wrong by future discoveries.[4] If it is right, however, something rather interesting follows: the earliest materials known are all of establishments actually in the tropical forests, and, what is more, they stretch (with large gaps) from one end to the other of the forests the civilized society came to cover.

These materials naturally do not present the difficulty the earliest materials for Egypt and for China do; that is to say, there is no difficult question whether they are materials left by a civilized society or not. The earliest known Middle American materials are part of a steadily developing series, just one of those series whose types change too rapidly and progressively to be the product of primitive societies; also, the process of conglomeration by which the social units in different places in a civilized society are drawn together is already shown in the types of their products. And in the Middle American Society that is a matter deserving particular attention because at all times, and especially at the relatively early time to which the remains in question belong, the different parts of the society were exceptionally widely scattered.[5] But there is a gap in the record before these remains, and it was at a time within the gap that the civilized society originated.

This tentative archaeological evidence acquires much greater weight when it is correlated with one of the leading features of the conglomerate myth: this is the great promi-

[4] MacNeish is in no wise dogmatic about the opinion. He offers, in fact, two possible interpretations of the typological data, one which makes the materials in the forest earlier and one which does not, and he then expresses his preference for the former.

[5] Cf. remarks of Willey and Phillips in *American Anthropologist*, LVII (1955), 767. I suspect that their theory is applicable to all civilized societies at their origins, but that there lies behind the phenomena they describe something we do not perceive.

nence, in all sorts of associations throughout the myth, of the rain deities. These are quite special to the society; no other civilized society has deities of the kind. It is hardly necessary to point out that a society whose cult puts rain deities in a high place, quantitatively in a higher place than all other deities, must receive its water supply directly, probably obtrusively, in the form of rain. This makes it far more likely that the civilization got its start in the tropical forest, where the rain is seasonal and torrential, than that it got it in the Valley of Mexico, for the valley people depended conspicuously on lake and river water as well as directly on rain. Not that this prevented them from also becoming rain worshippers; such religious unity is, however, usual—invariable I think—during the age of faith of a civilized society, and the religion takes its character from the region in which it and the society itself first arose.[6] Hence MacNeish's calculation that the known early remains in the forest regions are earlier than those in the highlands means also that the actual beginnings of the civilized society were in one of the forest regions, and that the society in all probability spread throughout those regions rather before it extended into the highlands.

Origin in the rain forest does not absolutely rule out agency of the rivers which run through the forest. The society has creation myths which begin with the primordial waters; that might be taken to signify origin in a flooded valley. There are two large river systems which run through the forest at the base of the Yucatan Peninsula, the Usumacinta system and the system of the Rio Grande de Chiapas. The former is well known as a main communication system through the society, and there were plenty of settlements beside it; but older settlements than any of them are known. The latter

[6] It is only necessary to think of such well known cases as Christianity and Islam to see how a religion formed in one environment can be communicated to another, taking with it all its characteristics of environmental origin.

river is hardly known archaeologically yet. It would, of course, be of great significance in the present discussion if originating settlements were to be discovered on one of these rivers, or on any of the shorter rivers which empty into the Gulf of Mexico or the Caribbean. But even if such settlements were found, they could not alter the fact that, quite a short time after its origin, the society was scattered all over the forest. Personally, I do not think such settlements will be found; I think the prominence of the rain gods means that rain water was from the beginning the water the society lived on and that any river water which was used was incidental.

We come, then, to the crucial question how the physiography of the Middle American Society, a tropical rain forest, could serve the society as an original environmental base in the same way as river valleys served other primary civilized societies. A tropical rain forest is not a river valley, but it has swamps as a river valley also does. The Middle American rain forest has, in fact, much swampland and many lakes. It has an excessive water supply for more than half the year, not merely at the inundation as a river valley has. Clearance of the wild vegetation in the rain forest was certainly a task similar to that in a river valley. But it was, in fact, a far greater task, as Eric Thompson has shown;[7] it was without question the most difficult material task which any primary civilized society encountered in its early days. As against this, water control was probably not a great task. The country is limestone country, and, although the sub-soil is not everywhere excessively porous, as the lakes and swamps plainly show, it is porous enough to keep floods down to something quite minor. Moreover, there is always water, for, apart from

[7] J. Eric S. Thompson, *The Rise and Fall of Maya Civilization* (Norman, 1954), pp. 23-26.

rivers and lakes, there is some rain even in the so-called dry months.

What this society never had was an automatic renewal of the cultivable land, such as the valley societies derived from the inundation. In fact, after the inordinately heavy task of clearing the tropical forest, the farmer had only two or three years use of the cleared land; he had then to move his fields elsewhere and clear the forest again. As against this, the land was fairly quickly restored when it reverted to forest. It may be, therefore, that after a few decades it could be cleared and used again, and a sort of circular movement from one site to another may have developed as the society grew. This, however, is pure guesswork; actually, we do not know how the society met this problem if indeed it met it in any way other than by abject submission. In any case, it cannot be overemphasized that the intermittent task of clearance was a very great burden; so also, however, was the task of water control, even quite elementary water control, in a valley society. Such burdens undoubtedly played their own part in the origin of civilized societies.

There is little difficulty in theory about the origin of the peoples who founded the Middle American Society. And it is fortunate that theoretical considerations are reliable in this instance—in the sense that they are self-evident—for there are no data connecting the earliest known settlers with peoples in other places who preceded them. There can be no doubt that the settlers came from the north, for that is where the land was drying out; it had been doing so for a long time— continuously, in fact, from the time of origin of agriculture and from several millennia before that.[8]

But there is a very large gap in the archaeological record before the earliest data about the civilized people, a gap which

[8] See above, Ch. 2, pp. 58-59.

occasions a lot of perplexity to the archaeologists.[9] As to that, however, it must be pointed out that the gap is, at least in its latter part and in the rain forest regions, quite to be expected: there, it simply means that the early civilized peoples were immigrants into the rain forest, just as we know that the founders of other civilized societies were immigrants into river valleys. The rain forest was an even less attractive place to primitive farmers than river valleys were, and farmers did not take refuge in either until they had to. We have, of course, yet to find record of the actual settlers in the forest, but it is most unlikely that primitives lived there before them. Mesolithics may merely have visited the forest to hunt in it; such people probably did not leave records there unless rarely of arrowheads.

But this supposition for the rain forest accounts only for the latter end of the gap in the record and only for the part of Middle America covered by the rain forest. For the rest of the territory—for a substantially larger territory than even this very broadly based civilized society covered—the earlier records are indeed extraordinarily scanty. The only early agricultural record is in the northeast corner of the territory in a cave in Tamaulipas, and that is of a people vastly different from the earliest peoples we know anywhere in the territory of the civilized society. The Tamaulipas people may very possibly not be ancestral to the peoples of the civilized society at all, although the earliest of them certainly antedate the civilized society by five hundred or more years—to about 2500 B.C. by a Carbon 14 reckoning.[10] Otherwise, there are records for all Middle America only of mesolithics, or, just possibly a few other early agriculturalists like those of Tamaulipas who have, however, left no signs of their agricul-

[9] E.g., Willey and Phillips, pp. 763-764.
[10] Libby, *Radiocarbon Dating*, p. 130, item C-587, 4445 ± 280 years ago.

ture.[11] Even these, mesolithics and others if any, are very few.

There is, I think, a probable explanation of all this in Paul Sears' findings about climate by means of comparative pollen analysis,[12] which serve in some measure to extend Antevs' findings to Middle America.[13] Both Sears and Antevs find a long dry period somewhat before the time when the civilized society arose; in the dry period all lakes and, presumably, rivers were much lower than they had become in early civilized times, for a wet period intervened before civilized times, and probably wetness, though lessening, continued into the very early civilized era. Sears thinks the establishments of the inhabitants in pre-civilized times were on the shores of the low lakes, and that the material remains of those establishments have long ago been carried away and destroyed by the higher water which has occurred since.

It may well prove, therefore, that we continue forever without actual record of the predecessors of the civilized peoples. Nevertheless, I think we may assume that the people who began the civilized society came from highland territory which still had water, but was then losing it. In fact, as in the western desert belt of the Old World, we should look to a region which was least dry, not to one most dry, for a source of population at so late a time in the desiccation process as the origin of a civilized society. There is no real indication of where such a region was, but Sears thinks the Lake Texcoco region was getting drier in an early period of the development of the civilized society; it could, therefore, already have been getting drier before the civilized society originated, and its excess of population could have migrated into the rain forest, where water was undiminished, or not appreciably diminished, and there have initiated the growth

[11] Willey and Phillips, pp. 751-752.
[12] See note 1 above.
[13] See Ch. 2, n. 53.

of the civilized society.[14] There is, of course, no doubt that primitives living where water was diminishing had an excess of population even while there was still water enough to show a damp climate in the pollen record. And besides the excess resulting from reduction of water there probably was one also from natural increase. We have not supposed that New World agriculture promoted increase in numbers as forcefully as Old World agriculture did, but there can be no doubt that New World agriculture brought about some increase in numbers.

If indeed the initiators of the civilized society, or their immediate ancestors, did live previously in the Lake Texcoco region, that could provide an explanation of the later importance of the region similar to the importance of the loess highlands of China in the Chinese Society. A connection with the valley may well have been maintained by the settlers in the forest. It is pretty clear that the latter created the new features of the society's religion (for which see Chapter 5), but they evidently communicated it back to those they had left behind in the valley, where it would certainly have some effective meaning, and they communicated also nearly every other novelty the civilization produced.

As to dates, the earliest Carbon 14 date we have is one for the Texcoco region, but, of course, for well after the beginning of the civilized society; it is for the "Early Zacatenco" remains, and it gives about the middle of the second millennium B.C.[15] If MacNeish is right, the earliest known remains

---

[14] Sears says that the "Archaic or Middle Cultures" enjoyed the benefit of a relatively humid climate (p. 57), but this must not be construed to mean that the "cultures" before them, the earliest civilized cultures in the valley and the primitive ones immediately before them, enjoyed a less humid climate; they must, in fact, have enjoyed a more humid one—a proposal which is quite consistent with what Sears says otherwise and is required by Antevs' opinions.

[15] Libby, p. 128, item C-196, 3310 ± 250 years ago; G. R. Willey, "The Prehistoric Civilizations of Nuclear America," *American Anthropologist*, LVII (1955), 573.

in the lowlands were earlier than that, and the beginning of the civilized society earlier again—probably about 2000 B.C.

Crete offers first the question of the source of the island's population. The earliest immigrants arrived there at a time difficult to fix, but probably not very long after the time of arrival of settlers in Egypt and Mesopotamia.[16] Those who went to Crete seem, most probably, to have come from Anatolia or, less probably, from Syria,[17] places which were at the time losing water supply and whose farming population was increasing. No great danger is involved in the voyage to Crete from the mainland, for the sea passage is sheltered by the islands of Rhodes, Karpathos, and Kasos. If the migrants were coasting along the shore of Asia Minor, they may very possibly have taken the route via those islands unintentionally, thinking they were still coasting, for each island is visible in good weather from the next. In any case, it is not surprising that peoples seeking new land for settlement should venture to sea as well as into river valleys they had not previously inhabited.

In short, there is no difficulty in explaining how Crete came to be inhabited by primitive farmers, or in relating their arrival there to changes in physical conditions which had to do with the resort of other primitive farmers to the river valleys.

But the civilized society did not take its rise on the first arrival of population in the island. That population was indeed a farming population with animals, but at first a very simple one, some of whom lived in caves and rock shelters. Before long, however, the progressive changes characteristic of civilized peoples begin to appear. As far as we know at present,

[16] See J.D.S. Pendlebury, *The Archaeology of Crete: An Introduction* (London, 1939), pp. 42-43.
[17] Pendlebury, pp. 37, 42.

there was at first a settlement on the site of the later palace at Knossos. It was on a knoll above the River Kairatos, which has some water all the year round, and in the course of time the settlement became very large. Actually, no other settlement of such a simple type is yet known in the island[18] although I think it is virtually certain that there were others.

The earliest settlement at Knossos has been described as "Lower Neolithic." It was followed by "Middle Neolithic" and "Upper Neolithic," and settlements of the two latter types spread into various places in the center and east of the island. In the progression of these types the early movement of the civilization is shown. The large settlement at Knossos looks like a reservoir of population from which other settlements, many of which were very small, may have been drawn. The island was not at all easy for such simple people to settle in. It is exceedingly mountainous, much of the land very high and much of it precipitous. And there is in the summer a grave shortage of water. The rivers are all small in so small an island, and in the summer most of them dry up. Like the Yucatan Peninsula in Middle America, the island has a limestone base, but the Cretan limestone is very porous, and no water lies for long.

There is in Crete no river valley remotely comparable with the great valleys in which the majority of the primary civilized societies have originated. Yet the unusual physiography of the island does produce a phenomenon which offers some analogy with a valley, a closer analogy than Middle America can be said to offer. This phenomenon consists in a number of plains lying between mountain ranges, the plains catching each year a new cover of alluvial soil brought down from the precipitous slopes of the mountains.[19] Most of them are in-

---

[18] Pendlebury, pp. 35, 37.

[19] See L. G. Allbaugh, *Crete: A Case Study of an Undeveloped Area* (Princeton, 1953), soil map opposite p. 286, for a conspectus of the soils of the island.

termount plains, entirely surrounded by mountains, or at least by higher land, and drained by sink-holes—called locally *chonoi*—through the limestone.[20] Because of this drainage, the plains have become plains and not lakes. In the winter and spring, however, they are heavily inundated with the run-off of rains and melting snows from the mountains. A few of the plains are drained by small streams,[21] hardly to be called rivers, but the effect of this is little different from drainage through the limestone sub-soil.

The whole island contains plains of this sort, but they are especially numerous, though very small,[22] in the Sitia Peninsula at the eastern end of the island. Many of the plains are too high for agriculture, but those up to about 3000 feet above sea level were used by the early settlers, and they are used still. Lasithi, or Psychro, the largest of the intermount plains, is just under 3000 feet high. It is some forty miles from the eastern end of the island (which is only 160 miles long in all) and about half way across it from north to south. It is adjacent to Mount Dicte, one of the great mountains of the island. Lasithi is, in fact, girdled in a semi-circle by Mount Dicte, from whose slopes has come most of the plain's covering.[23]

The Plain of Messara is far larger than Lasithi. Messara is a special case. It lies in the south center of the island between the Ida Range on the north and the Asterousia Range (now called Kophinos) on the south. It is drained by the River Lethaios, one of the larger rivers of the island, running from east to west and emptying into the sea. The Lethaios is the one Cretan river which might be taken—more accurately, mistaken—for the river in whose valley the civilized society originated. It is not in the least comparable with the great

[20] Allbaugh, p. 47; Pendlebury, pp. 5-6.
[21] Allbaugh, p. 47.
[22] Too small, apparently, to appear on Allbaugh's map. Pendlebury mentions Zyros, Katalioni, and Lamnioni (p. 6).
[23] Pendlebury, pp. 5-6.

rivers in whose valleys other civilized societies have arisen, and yet its relatively puny waters may have been the first thing which attracted settlers to the Messara, and settlers who learned the special character of the Messara Plain may, or their descendants may, the more easily have come to understand the character and advantages of the numerous small upland plains. But that is a speculation. The Lethaios, in fact, alters the character of the Plain of Messara only a little; it merely gives the plain a special advantage. Like the other plains, the Messara receives huge masses of humus-laden soil from the mountain slopes flanking it; that is the real advantage it has for primitive farmers. As a result, it is and always has been one of the most fertile and prosperous areas of land in Crete.

The meaning of all this for the origin of the civilized society becomes clear, I believe, from the fact that the bulk of the population in the neolithic periods sought the intermount plains and the Messara. In those periods the population was in no wise dependent on the sea, as it became later. In fact, although there were ports, most settlements seem to have been placed as far from the sea as possible.[24] It was the plains with their reliable water supply and their fertility which afforded refuge to hard pressed farming peoples.

We get virtually no aid in determining the mode of origin of Cretan civilization from myth. There is indeed in the great body of Greek mythology quite a lot about Crete, but what is recognizable as such relates to Crete in its later days, the days of the "Thalassocracy" of Minos, or still later. It is very likely that Greek mythology also contains material reconstituted from Cretan mythology—that is to say, from the Cretan conglomerate myth as it was at the origin of the Cretan Society itself—but there is no way at all of identifying that

[24] Pendlebury, pp. 15-16, 35, 277; R. Matton, *La Crète antique* (Athens, Greece, 1955), pp. 13, 16.

at present. Greek mythology is related to all of the mythologies of the earlier Near East—which is in no wise unusual and, in fact, is perfectly natural. It appears to contain a good deal of Mesopotamian origin, but this may be deceptive, for we do not know that similar material was not in Cretan sources. There is not a thing that I can find in Greek myth which looks as if it described primeval physical conditions in the island of Crete. Just conceivably, the Pelasgian creation myth with its initial division of sky from sea, or the idea of Oceanus girdling the world,[25] reflects the importance of the sea to islanders, but the connection is very tenuous and speculative. In any case, these ideas could do no more than confirm the origin of a civilized society in the island, and we have decided on other grounds that that occurred.

Conditions at the origin of the Cretan Society were, then, as follows: the island is small, its cultivable land (for quasi-primitives, at least) scanty, its water supplies in most places entirely insufficient; as a consequence, its people sought the few regions in which they could survive at a certain price, and found that, in doing so, they not only survived but prospered. The soil of the plains, renewed every year in greater and greater new deposits as the inhabitants cut down the trees on the mountain sides,[26] gave their fields the same perpetual fertility as the annual inundation gave to fields in the river valleys; the price to be paid was that the people had to find ways of protecting themselves from the spring floods[27]

[25] See Robert Graves, *The Greek Myths*, Penguin Books, I (Baltimore, 1955), 27-31.

[26] Cf. Pendlebury, p. 6.

[27] See G. Perrot, *L'Ile de Crète* (Paris, 1867), p. 117, for the effects of the floods on the Lasithi Plain a century ago when there was apparently inadequate water control; I am not at all sure, however, that Perrot's description of the physical phenomenon is quite correct. Water control is inadequate in the plain today; see Allbaugh, p. 261. I think it likely that water control was better in early days when the settlers were getting themselves established. There are plenty of other places, Iran and parts of

and the summer droughts, from the latter presumably by preserving some of the flood waters and making full use of springs and wells.[28]

There is an obvious analogy, with differences of course, between this situation and that of the river valleys, and there cannot be any doubt that this was the material foundation on which the Cretan Society began to arise. But it did not long remain solely upon this foundation. Evidently, the combined resources of the plains of Crete were not equal to those of a river valley, or alternatively, the attractions of the sea as a source of sustenance were greater, or more obvious, than heroic schemes of irrigation, such as the valley societies developed in later stages of their history. The seaports became more and more important as the Cretan civilization grew, and they soon overtook Lasithi and the lesser upland plains as centers of population and of the high culture.[29] It is not that the plains were deserted; on the contrary, they continued to be thickly inhabited and to be an important source of food, while Messara long retained its position as a leading center in every sense. The society grew, however, with a powerful momentum, eventually finding in the sea and across the sea the preponderant resources to sustain itself.

There are no Carbon 14 dates for the history of Crete. There are only a series of generally accepted conventional dates for its archaeological periods, and for origins there is really nothing to go on. I shall merely suggest, therefore, that the earliest settlers landed somewhat earlier than 3000 B.C.[30]

For some of the river valley societies we have found that the early settlers made preliminary lodgments, in proximity

---

Sind, for example, where water control was much better in very early times than it is now.

[28] For the importance of these, see below, Ch. 5, p. 153.

[29] Pendlebury. p. 47.   [30] See Ch. 1, n. 3.

to the valleys but not in them, before taking the plunge into the valleys themselves. It is possible that establishments somewhere in the Valley of Mexico served the early settlers in Middle America in this way; such possible establishments have been compared above with the establishments of the proto-Chinese in the loess highlands of North China.

The case of Crete contains a single suggestive datum in this connection, the long sustained practice on the part of the population in the neolithic periods of living in caves and rock-shelters.[31] There is no doubt that the practice was a reversion, for, even in the very early settlement at Knossos, there were built structures of some sort; in later neolithic times there were structures at Phaistos in the Plain of Messara and at Magasa at the extreme eastern end of the island[32] and perhaps in other places we do not know of. I am therefore inclined to think the caves and shelters were temporary resorts at a time when temporariness of living arrangements was still an important factor in survival; that the population may have lived in them only for a part of the year, when its energies were fully employed otherwise than on building; and that at other times it retired to other places, including those three where building is known to have occurred.[33] But there may, of course, be some other explanation of the reversion to caves and rock-shelters.

The clue to the likeness and the difference between the valley and the non-valley environments of the primary civilized societies is clearest from the standpoint of the preliminary lodgments the earliest settlers made: they went in search of water, and where they found it in sufficient quantities they

[31] Pendlebury, pp. 277, 279.   [32] Pendlebury, pp. 44-45.
[33] Such temporariness would by no means be unique, but other possible cases are not sure either. For example, it is not sure whether the Tasian-Badarian settlements on the eastern edge of the Nile Valley were permanent settlements; they may also have been merely temporary encampments made in the course of seeking preliminary lodgment in the valley region.

settled, however difficult the conditions of settlement were. That river valleys were often the places chosen is no surprise. Even the Lethaios in Crete may have served as a link in the approach toward a permanent water supply which came, however, from quite a different source. In fact, I think it rather more probable that that insignificant stream did so than that the rivers of Middle America did, for in Middle America rain-water is far more obviously in evidence than it is in Crete; farming settlers reaching the rain forest could not have failed to see its possibilities, even if they were at the same time appalled by the task the possibilities imposed.

The combination of possibilities with tasks, of opportunities with obstacles, is the largest aspect of the common material conditions at the origin of all the primary civilized societies. In Middle America water was free and easily manageable, but the soil was obtained only at the price of the terrible and almost continuous burden of clearing the tropical forest. In all the valleys and in Crete soil was free, but the management of the waters presented problems of great difficulty, while in some valleys the protection of the fields against the wild vegetation reflected, always in lesser degree, the forest problem of Middle America.

It is of particular interest that climate is not among the like material conditions at the origin of the primary civilized societies. In the last chapter it was found that one society arose in a temperate climate, the others in sub-tropical climates. It now appears that two, the Chinese and Cretan societies, arose in temperate climates; that four, the Egyptian, Mesopotamian, Indian, and Andean societies, arose in subtropical climates; and that one, the Middle American Society, arose in a tropical climate. The inference is quite unmistakable without enquiry into any lesser details of climate differences: climate as such was not a factor in the origin of civilized societies.

Finally, for the scholar the combination of close likenesses with large differences in the material evidence, here in the physical evidence, is rather a useful lesson. It is very important that most of the primary civilized societies originated in river valleys, but not so important as to require that such societies could not have originated elsewhere. The realities of the processes of human history do not necessarily lie conspicuous upon the surface of the evidence. In fact, I think they rarely do so, whether the evidence is of a material-physical kind, or of some other kind. As a matter of fact, the pattern here shown, of a majority of cases of a historic phenomenon rather closely resembling one another coupled with a minority apparently entirely different, is quite a usual one in history. Underlying such differences there are probably always likenesses, but the likenesses are not always discernible to us, as they are in the material conditions of origin of the primary civilized societies.

We pass now from material conditions of origin to conditions which subsisted at the time of origin in the minds of the men who created the civilized societies. These bring us into contact with a new order of realities underlying the immediate evidence. Those realities also show surprisingly close likenesses.

THE NEW RELIGIONS

THE material circumstances of man's original settlement in the sites of the primary civilized societies have now been surveyed and, among those circumstances, particularly the physiography of the sites. In a materialist interpretation of history this survey would cover the explanation of the origin of the societies. But this is not a materialist interpretation.

In Chapter 1 it was argued that every primary civilized society had, at or about the time of its origin, a new religion.[1] In this chapter the rise of these religions is substantiated. The new religion was indeed in every case compounded in part of old elements, but also of important new ones, and with the religion went charismatic leadership of the society by persons who came soon to be looked upon as priests, or possibly later as gods. The religions give a part, a very large part, of the explanation of the origin of the societies.

Each religion arose as a means of enabling the people of its society to survive. Later and increasingly, it became a means of directing the society's energies towards particular ends thought important and advantageous by its leaders. But we shall not be concerned here with those later events. Our enquiry begins logically with what has already been settled

[1] Ch. 1, pp. 14-16.

about the primary civilized societies, their special need for water. Fortunately, it is possible to show clearly, even conclusively, for most of the societies at their origin that religion was vitally concerned with the need for water. Water was, of course, the essential means of the societies' survival, and we shall find that it was the main aim of religion in the Egyptian, Mesopotamian, Middle American, and Andean societies, probably in the Indian and Chinese societies, and very possibly in the Cretan Society to secure water and establish in men's minds the appropriate and necessary devotion to it.

Egypt and Mesopotamia may be considered together and comparatively. Both societies had gods of the water, but gods who differed about as much as they were alike. Enki in Mesopotamia[2] and Osiris in Egypt[3] were both immanent in water. They were both water which was in the earth or came to the earth: they were chthonic gods. What they did for crops or otherwise for the increase of things, they did in the earth or on the earth. They were both creators, Enki rather broadly so of crops, and also of pasture and of other things, Osiris more especially of the grain, Egyptian theology developing early (but in the course of a fairly long time) much ingenious detail as to how Osiris brought the grain into existence—how he actually was the grain as well as the water. Enki and Osiris reflect the difference between the waters of the habitats of the two societies. It was emphasized that Enki was fresh water, for the Mesopotamians were well acquainted, and by no means always pleasantly, with the salt water of the

[2] Thorkild Jacobsen in Frankfort, Frankfort, Wilson, Jacobsen, and Irwin, *The Intellectual Adventure of Ancient Man* (Chicago, 1946), pp. 146-148.

[3] Henri Frankfort, *Kingship and the Gods: A Study of Ancient Near Eastern Religion as the Integration of Society and Nature* (Chicago, 1948), pp. 190-195 and *passim*.

Persian Gulf.[4] Enki was the river water, but similarly the water of wells and springs and rain-water as well. Egypt had little rain. It had a rain-god, Min of Koptos, but he was not the great water-god. Osiris was narrowly and specially the Nile water.[5] In fact, he was the inundation, he was immanent in the inundation, he floated in it, and his annual arrival in it was awaited by Egyptians with joyful anticipation.

For present purposes it is very significant that both Enki and Osiris can be traced back a long way in the history of their respective societies; in fact, both may well go back to origins. Enki in his capacity as a local god—and all the great gods of Egypt and Mesopotamia, and certainly of other societies also, had their local origins—belonged to Eridu, which we know to have been the oldest of the Mesopotamian cities. There, among the earliest remains, has been found a temple, almost certainly Enki's temple, which is the simple, crude prototype of all Mesopotamian temples. At al Ubaid, probably the next oldest settlement in Mesopotamia, there are also signs that Enki was worshipped. It looks, therefore, as if he was at least one of the original gods of the society, possibly the only important one.[6]

Osiris figures prominently in the Memphite Theology, a

---

[4] Lees' and Falcon's work (G. M. Lees and N. L. Falcon, "The Geographical History of the Mesopotamian Plains," *Geographical Journal,* CXVIII [1952], 24-39) makes it seem likely that at least some of the major floods of Mesopotamia were transgressions of the Gulf waters rather than excessive river inundations.

[5] He does appear as other waters occasionally and rarely, but these are probably not more than the product of enthusiastic imaginings of theologians; see Frankfort, *Kingship,* p. 191.

[6] I follow the opinion of Frankfort (*The Birth of Civilization in the Near East,* Bloomington, 1954, pp. 47-48), who thinks there was at Eridu "continuity, not only of architectural development, but of worship" and that the remains at al Ubaid of fishbones in the offerings to the god mean that that god was Enki since fish were associated with him and were offered to him in later times. If Enki was in fact the only important god in the earliest days in Mesopotamia, this does not point to an early monotheism, or anything of the sort; see p. 163 below.

document relating to the unification of Egypt a little after 3000 B.C. by Menes, the conqueror from the south. It is, in fact, clear that Osiris came from the south along with Menes, and was set up as a prominent god of the society at Menes' new capital, Memphis. There is good reason to suppose that before his establishment at Memphis Osiris had been local god, as he continued throughout Egyptian history to be, at Abydos, a city of the This Nome, Menes' family state, and that he had already been established there for a long time before the unification.[7] That brings Osiris back to a time significantly near Egyptian origins. If, indeed, he goes back actually to origins, he may then have been a chieftain, a king, a god-king—for all Egyptian kings were gods—and so one of those charismatic leaders who took part in the very foundation of the society. There is, as far as I can judge the scanty and vague evidence, about an equal chance that, in his capacity as fertilizing water, Osiris was of Asiatic or of African origin. If he was of Asiatic origin, he was very likely brought to Egypt by the Gerzeans, the latest of the participants in the formation of the Egyptian Society to arrive in Egypt. If he was of African origin, he must have come to Egypt earlier than the Gerzeans, perhaps with the very first agricultural settlers.[8] He could have been of dual origin, even in his capac-

---

[7] I again follow Frankfort whose reasoning here is masterly even if it is not necessarily final; see *Kingship*, pp. 201-203. Mrs. Elise J. Baumgartel (*The Cultures of Prehistoric Egypt*, London, 1947, p. 4), citing A. Rusch ("Die Stellung des Osiris im theologischen System von Heliopolis," *Der Alte Orient*, XXIV, Heft 1, 1924, p. 11), says that nothing is known of Osiris before the Fifth Dynasty. Rusch wrote before the publication of Kurt Sethe's elucidation of the Memphite Theology (*Dramatische Texte zu altägyptischen Mysterienspielen*, Untersuchungen zur Gesch. u. Altertumskunde Ägyptens, X, Leipzig, 1928, pp. 1-80). To repeat Rusch on this matter in 1947 is an egregious scholarly blunder.

[8] The idea that he came from Asia is an old established one, but those who think he did usually think also that he was first established in Egypt at Busiris, or somewhere in the Delta; see, e.g., H. Kees, *Der Götterglaube im alten Ägypten: Mitteilungen der Vorderasiatisch-ägyptischen Gesellschaft*, XLV (Leipzig, 1941), 213 and *passim*. I am fully persuaded by

ity as a water-god. He had other capacities also, and, if all his capacities are considered together, he was almost certainly of dual origin. In any case, it is hard to resist the impression that he was a very early deity in Egypt, just possibly the earliest.

It does not appear likely that the water cults of Egypt and Mesopotamia, vital as they certainly were to the societies' establishment and survival, actually laid down any rules for water control, still less for anything which can be called irrigation. It is, indeed, usually assumed that diking and dredging began in Mesopotamia as soon as settlements were made there; canal building followed later. I have added to this assumption the further one that the settlers knew a good deal about such things before their arrival; they probably arrived prepared to undertake them. At a much later time, irrigation *was* in fact a prescription of religion, but it was an incidental, not an essential, feature of it, not the subject of official ritual, or of doctrine.

For Egypt the question is less simple. The Gerzeans began to drain the swamps so that, if Osiris as water-god was of earlier origin, he did not require anything of that sort. If he came, in this capacity, with the Gerzeans, there is—in knowledge available at present—not much likelihood that water control was required in his cult, just an outside chance that it was.[9]

Frankfort that Osiris began his career in Egypt at Abydos (see previous note), but cannot quite believe that the myth of Osiris is so completely unlike the myths of the dying vegetation gods of Asia as Frankfort avers. There is always the possibility too—though I do not think so in this instance—that the African ideas Frankfort finds in Egyptian thought about kingship, deity, and vegetal growth were first Egyptian and thereafter diffused elsewhere in Africa. For Frankfort's view of Osiris as a deity of wholly African origin, see *Kingship*, pp. 33-35, 198-200.

[9] Frankfort, *Birth*, p. 43 and n. 5; G. Brunton, *The Badarian Civilization* (London, 1948), p. 48; cf. Baumgartel, *op.cit.*, p. 46; cf. also Ch. 3, n. 68 above.

I think, then, that water control is to be seen, for Egypt and Mesopotamia, as a practical undertaking which arose as soon as the need for it was understood. Irrigation in any large meaning of the term is not in question; that came after several centuries, when the society was compelled to extend its lands to feed a growing population. At origins, elementary water control no doubt came naturally enough to peoples whose concern about water supply was so great that it entered in an important way into their religions. But the religions laid down only the sacred, magical, beneficent quality of water; the doctrine must have been that water was itself a deity, that it was an element in deity, or that a god gave it and guarded it, or something of that sort; after the god had done his part—and he might need to be cajoled or compelled to do it—it was for men to get busy and make the most profitable and safest use of the water which they had received.

The Andean, Chinese, Indian, and Middle American societies may be considered as another group of societies related to one another. But their special relationship is not perhaps of much intrinsic importance, for it is merely their symbolism that they shared. All of them shared the serpent, dragon, or serpent-dragon as water-symbol. There was also a feline animal as symbol of the earth,[10] this latter being of great importance in the Andean Society, of less importance in the Middle American Society, of somewhat doubtful meaning in the Chinese Society, and, as far as I know, entirely lacking in the Indian Society. But, if the common symbolism is not important in itself, it proves to have great importance here in throwing light upon the earliest beliefs about water and earth in China. Otherwise, the remarkable thing about these four societies is the fundamental similarity between the

[10] The more or less common symbolism of the societies is explained below; pp. 155-158.

water-earth elements in their religion and the same elements in Mesopotamian and Egyptian religion—a similarity, the reader may be interested to know, which was as astonishing to me when I first came upon it as it will possibly be to him. With the similarity there go, of course, dissimilarities, and the similarity with the two Near Eastern societies is greater in the case of the Andean Society than in the case of the Chinese, Indian, and Middle American societies. For that reason the Andean Society will be studied first of the four.

The first thing to notice about the Andean society is that true irrigation occupies the same place in its history as we have supposed it to occupy in the history of Egypt and Mesopotamia. In chronology irrigation comes in the Andean Society as late as, or later than, in the Egyptian Society—at least five hundred years after the origin of the Andean Society;[11] hence it cannot have had a place in the original religious doctrine. And this in spite of the fact that the Andean irrigation system, when fully developed, was probably the most complex and efficient of any in the primary civilized societies. As in the Mesopotamian Society, however, when irrigation was developed, it came under religious sanction.[12] There must, of course, have been some management of the waters in the Andean Society from an early time, from the origin of the society probably, but, as in the Egyptian and Mesopotamian cases, the evidence gives nothing about that in the prescriptions of religion.

Since the Andean Society has the distinction of being the

[11] The date is not at all exact; there is no way of fixing it closely at present; see Gordon R. Willey, *Prehistoric Settlement Patterns in the Virú Valley, Peru*, Smithsonian Institution, Bureau of American Ethnology, Bulletin 155 (Washington, 1953), p. 362.

[12] W. D. Strong and C. Evans, Jr., *Cultural Stratigraphy in the Virú Valley, Northern Peru: The Formative and Florescent Periods* (New York, 1952), p. 199.

only non-literate society, we do not have for events in its earliest days the valuable hindsight from later written evidence that we have for the Mesopotamian and Egyptian societies and to a lesser extent for the Chinese and the Middle American. Oddly enough and most providentially, however, we do have another form of record, and that from an earlier date than any comparable record except the early temple at Eridu in Mesopotamia, which in any case does not give as precise and dependable data as the Andean record does. The Andean record consists of sculptures and reliefs of sacred subjects in temples and of a zoomorphic-anthropomorphic pottery used to represent sacred matters. All these representations show the Andean cat-god, the chthonic deity, as principal and, in association with him, the serpent which stands for water.

The sculptures suggest that the god's chief function has to do with water,[13] but the pots—which are of the very early Cupisnique period—are more subtle than this and so more explicit. Two of them are described by their discoverer, Rafael Larco Hoyle, as "la serpiente felinica," and they exhibit a merging in the same figure of feline and herpetoid characters, the one showing the serpent rather predominant, the other the cat.[14] A third one shows a humanoid cat-face—

[13] Two from the temple of Chavín de Huantar are figured, respectively, in *Handbook of South American Indians, II: The Andean Civilizations*, ed. Julian H. Steward, Smithsonian Institution, Bureau of American Ethnology, Bulletin 143 (Washington, 1946), p. 83, fig. 1, and in Rafael Larco Hoyle, *Los Cupisniques*, Sociedad Geográfica Americana (Buenos Aires, 1945), p. 3 = *Revista Geográfica Americana*, xxvii (1947), p. 89. The first of these very much stylized figures is of the deity front-view, standing in human fashion; eight serpents stand out on each side of him, forming a part of the upper décor, and two emerge from each side of his waist. The other figure, which is scarcely at all anthropomorphic, gives a side view of the deity with serpent heads projecting from the outer lines of the body at various points and two heads with necks projecting from the side of the deity's mouth.

[14] *Los Cupisniques* (Buenos Aires), p. 11, top figure, and p. 10 = *Revista Geogr. Am.*, xxvii, 97, top figure, and 96; *Handbook of South American*

nearly all representations of the cat are to some extent human-ized—having the eyebrow formed of one complete serpent and the head of another serpent emerging from the mouth.[15] We can read these serpent symbols as if they were glyphs, which they almost are: the eyebrow serpent is the water on the face of the earth, presumably the rivers, and the serpent emerging from the earth-god's mouth the water which comes out of the earth, spring water and well water.[16] They could, in fact, be none other than these, for rain is extremely rare on the Andean coast and not beneficial to men.[17]

The closeness of the resemblance to the corresponding idea for early Mesopotamia is truly amazing. The name of the Mesopotamian water deity, Enki, means literally "lord of the earth." "From the earth," says Jacobsen, "come the life-giving sweet waters, the water in wells, in springs, in rivers; and in very early times these 'waters which wander in the earth' seem to have been considered as part of its being, an aspect among many aspects under which it might be viewed."[18]

Indians, II, Plate 64a, and Plate 63d. The first has a pair of serpent heads projecting from the pot, the features being curiously modified so that they are to an appreciable extent feline as well as herpetoid. In the other only one side of the pot is illustrated, and that side appears to be half the face of the cat-god, the principal features and folds of the face being formed of a serpent's coils.

[15] Larco Hoyle, *Los Cupisniques* (Lima, 1941—a publication distinct from the one of the same title cited in the two previous notes), cover design and figs. 212, 213, and 214, three aspects of the pot.

[16] Cf. the two serpent heads projecting from the side of the deity's mouth in the second of the two figures described in n. 13.

[17] The Andean Society, at early period, had, so far as we know, shown no signs of any interest in rain. The "weeping god," who certainly signifies reverence for a rain-giver, was a god of the mountain regions. If the society had by Cupisnique times begun to extend into the mountains, it would seem that those regions were not yet of any cultural consequence, so that their ideas had not yet begun to penetrate to the coast, which (according to the views I hold) was the original base of the civilized society; cf. T. A. Joyce, in *Essays and Studies Presented to William Ridgeway* (Cambridge, 1913), p. 368.

[18] *Intellectual Adventure*, p. 146. In historical times (for which there

The times to which the Andean pots refer were, as has been remarked, early times, and what Jacobsen says would seem to be as good a description of the early Andean, as of the early Mesopotamian, feeling about water and earth.

The "terraqueous deity" of the Andean Society, as Larco appropriately calls him,[19] must have been god of agriculture already in the Cupisnique period; he certainly was so later.[20] In this he resembles Osiris more than Enki, for Enki, while retaining his aqueous (not his terraqueous) function, developed as a secondary character ingenuity and astuteness in counsel. Another resemblance of Andean to Egyptian thought is evident in an Andean cat-frog-vegetal figure which had to do with the infiltration of water into plants,[21] much as Osiris infiltrated into the grain. This Andean figure may represent a special function of the cat-god, or it may represent a special daimon, distinct from the cat-god; but any distinction is one with only a minor difference.

Funerary pottery of a later period in Andean history shows an understanding that river water came from the mountains in the east of the society's territory.[22] This perception may have been connected with the rise of belief in a Supreme Deity who had his seat in the mountains.[23] Other funerary pots seem to show that water was revered, or at least appreciated, as the source of the society's supply of fish[24]—a sufficiently obvious idea indeed and one shared with the Mesopotamian Society; but the idea was of special importance to the Andean Society, for the society had inherited a rather large depend-

---

are written records) the form of the name is the only surviving evidence of the intimacy of the relationship of water and earth.

[19] "La divinidad terráquea"; *Los Cupisniques* (Lima, 1941), p. 151.

[20] Strong and Evans, p. 199.

[21] Larco in *Handbook of South American Indians*, ii, 172.

[22] Strong and Evans, pp. 163-164.

[23] Larco, *Los Cupisniques* (Lima, 1941), p. 151; *Handbook of South American Indians*, ii, 171-173.

[24] Strong and Evans, pp. 163-164, 200.

ence upon fish from the pre-agricultural primitives who had preceded it on the Pacific coast. Whether or not the source of the water in the mountains, and reverence for the mountains and for a Supreme Deity living in them, formed a part of belief in the Andean Society's early days, it is impossible to say, but there is some chance that they did, even though the earliest known pots which convey the ideas date to as much as 800 years later than the Cupisnique pottery.[25]

Such special physical features as the Andean mountains may, then, have affected belief and have caused it to diverge from the beliefs of other valley societies. But among such physical features the multiplicity of the Andean rivers is not obviously in evidence. Perhaps, then, this difference was not an effective one at the origin of the valley societies. Rather, Egypt was the unusual case among them since its river was obtrusively single and continuous. The Euphrates and the Tigris were not single even if—which we do not know—they already flowed together then before they entered the Persian Gulf. Besides, the Kerkhah was probably known to the proto-Mesopotamians, as perhaps were also other lesser streams coming down from the Iranian scarp to the Persian Gulf. The Euphrates may consequently have been just the one of several rivers which the settlers happened to choose first. The insignificant tributaries of the Indus which run down from the Kirthars and enter the river from the west on its lower course are at least much more than the dry wadies of the Nile, while the great tributaries flowing from the east on the upper course of the river, the Sutlej, the Ravi, the Chenab, and the Jehlam, must have affected opinion as soon as their existence became known to the Indian peoples. But, even if their existence was long unknown, the Great Mihran was probably a sister river which must soon have become known.

[25] By Carbon 14 dates C-75 (2665 ± 200 years) and C-619 (1838 ± 190 years ago) ; Libby, *Radiocarbon Dating*, 2nd ed. (Chicago, 1955), p. 133.

In northern Peru there are also several rivers. We do not happen to know which one the settlers chose first, but probably one was earlier than the rest.[26] Which one it was may not be of much importance. Their multiplicity must have had some influence on the settlers' minds, at least as soon as they spread from the first river to others.

The singularity of the Nile may, therefore, be the special phenomenon, among the physical peculiarities affecting the four valley societies considered here, which should attract our attention. Thus, it would not at all surprise me if the singularity of the Nile was the reason why Egyptian water worship came to be concentrated upon the single annual inundation which the whole society must have experienced more or less together. The single, common experience may well have had special influence upon the society's early thought, leading it to a feeling about water somewhat different from that which arose in the primary civilized societies established in the valleys of several rivers at once. There will be a little more to say on this subject when the case of the Chinese Society is considered.

For the Chinese Society's early religious feelings about water there are both literary and artifactual records, the latter of a character in general like those for the Andean Society. It would seem at first consideration, then, that information about the Chinese Society ought to be better than that for the three societies studied until now. But this is not so. The Chinese artifacts, quite numerous bronzes and a little pottery, marble, and jade carving, are far later in the society's career than the Andean pots and carvings, and they are also,

---

[26] There is no strong reason why the ultimate origin should be found very near to the Cupisnique region, which is in the Chicama river drainage, for the Cupisnique remains, though very early, are not by any means the earliest remains. See above, Ch. 3, pp. 102-103 and references there given.

perhaps because they are late, comparatively inexplicit. As for the literature, although it professes again and again to explain the society's origin, the very earliest material in it was written two millennia or so later than that event, and the explanation has lost most of its value. It is, in fact, not for the explanation that the literature is useful here, but for the record it gives of survivals.

But mere lapse of time is not the real trouble with the literature; the literature belongs to the second cycle[27] of the society's history and the profound changes as the society declined and then revived at the transition from the first to the second cycle drew an opaque veil between the conditions of the first cycle and the writings of the second.[28] The literature is largely devoted to religion and mythology, in which matters the greatest changes between the two cycles occurred. It is the religion of the second cycle which the literature describes, and it is in that later religion that the survivals from the first cycle are found.

Broadly speaking, the literature shows Chinese religion

[27] The concept of cyclical development of civilized societies is explained in Ch. I, pp. 6-7.

[28] Some of the literary material for the origins of the Egyptian and Mesopotamian societies derives from the second cycles in the history of those societies, but by no means all of it does in either case. Creel propounds a hypothesis—most instructive for the present purpose, a purpose which Creel did not have in mind and whose very validity I daresay he would reject—that the early Chou government of China issued garbled versions of the earlier literature and destroyed the authentic documents (*Studies in Early Chinese Culture*, First Series, Baltimore, 1937, pp. 89-93). The early Chou government was a government early in the second cycle. If Creel's hypothesis is correct, then, it gives the reason why no literary material for the first cycle has been found.

Much of the "early" Chinese literature is, in fact, of a late date in the second cycle, a date after the age of the "hundred schools" (6th-4th centuries B.C.), a Renaissance-Reformation age in which most that was written had special ethical or other purposes quite irrelevant to conditions at the beginning of any cycle, primary or later, in the history of a civilized society. These books in themselves create confusion whenever they deal with origins, which they do not seldom.

141

in the second cycle still exalting agriculture to the summit of importance. Such things as the spring ceremony of "opening the soil" performed for the whole society by the emperor and his chief officials, but also by the heads of every local unit even down to the village for their respective units, are quite typical of agriculturally centered civilized societies. But we want to know specifically about water. There are innumerable signs of its importance in the huge number of stories involving dragons or serpents,[29] but many of these have been re-interpreted to new purposes in the new cycle and can be, are in fact, misleading. Nevertheless, their popularity is, I feel sure, a sign of the importance of water, for they constantly betray their earlier meaning in various of their details.

Two rather striking examples of this are the folk tales of the spring celebrations respectively in the principalities of Lu and Cheng.[30] The Lu celebration was a dragon-dance which began with the dancers actually *in* the waters of the River Yi; the dancers then emerged onto the bank, and the ceremony concluded with the water sacrifice, held in the area on the river bank traditional for the purpose. Obviously, such a ceremony was a magical means of inducing a sufficient inundation.[31] There were other dragon dances, but the Lu and

[29] Creel (*Studies,* pp. 237-239) discusses the relevance of the dragon symbol to rain, but only to rain, not to water in any other form.

[30] These were feudal principalities which traditionally were formed early in the first millennium B.C., during the age of faith of the second cycle in the history of China. The spring celebrations are, of course, vastly older than that, and have merely been assigned to the feudal principalities because the accounts of them were recorded when the principalities existed.

[31] The Lu tale is in the *Analects of Confucius* (*Lun Yu*), discussions in which he had taken part afterwards collected by his followers. The Cheng tale is in the *Shih Ching* (*Book of Poetry*), one of the two most ancient of the Chinese so-called Classics, but in a late passage of it. In neither of the sources is there a word about inundations, nor, as far as I know, in any of the writings about them by the fairly numerous later Chinese commentators. In the Cheng case this is not surprising. It is, however, to be noted that scholars of today, in commenting on the stories, have not thought of the point, or have not thought it worth mentioning;

the Cheng ones have a special importance, for they are the only clear evidence I know of in the history of China to show that a river inundation was ever thought beneficent. We shall return to that matter below.

Regular household sacrifices to the god of the wells and the god of the impluvium (the cistern to catch rainwater running off the roof) show a continuing popular religious concern with well-water and rain. There was also an official sacrifice for rain performed by emperors and kings in the summer, the only season in which North China gets an appreciable quantity of rain, and that usually insufficient. There were, too, among the official deities two shadowy personages, who received no very specific attention, called "Master of the Rain" and "Count of the Wind." That is about all the literature tells. Hou T'u, god of the land, hardly looks like earth, as we have found earth in the other three societies; Hou T'u had developed too much into a feudal, or at least a territorial-political, deity although in his background there are complications which may hide something different.[32]

This is not perhaps an inconsiderable sum to distil out of literature written thousands of years after the time in which we are interested. We shall get more, however, from the artifactual remains even though many of these were no older

consider particularly M. Granet, *Fêtes et chansons anciennes de la Chine*, 2nd ed. (Paris, 1929), pp. 155-164, 167-176, where the meaning of the stories is fully discussed; cf. H. Maspero, *Mélanges posthumes sur les religions et l'histoire de la Chine, I: Les religions chinoises* (Paris, 1950), pp. 156-160.

[32] See Bernhard Karlgren, "Some Fecundity Symbols in Ancient China," *Bulletin of the Museum of Far Eastern Antiquities*, II (1930), pp. 10-17, esp. p. 16, where it is proposed that the deity of earth was of dual origin, one part being a female deity (presumably, like a Near Eastern earth-mother), the two having been amalgamated by Chou scholars. If something like this did happen, I should be inclined to attribute it rather to early Chou politician-priests, seeking to make the Chou political authority over the land and the magnates established on it more secure.

than the literature and the few that were older were only a few centuries older. The main reason for their greater usefulness is not, I believe, the greater antiquity of some of them, but instead the far greater imperviousness of the craftsman's practices than the writer's to the inroads of theory, creative and re-creative, of the new theology of the second cycle.

In moving over to the craftsman's sphere of work, then, the first thing that strikes the student is the positive ubiquity of the *lung*, the aquatic dragon or serpent. It is vastly more pervasive than it is in the literature, and its meaning is supported and extended by the *lei wên* and *yün wên* motifs, which represent thunder and rain.[33] But the meanings of these symbols are well known. The special center of interest and of the designs themselves is the *t'ao-t'ieh*, rendered literally the "glutton" figure, which appears on almost all the oldest bronzes,[34] the few marbles,[35] and with declining frequency, but still significantly, on the many jades.[36] The *t'ao-t'ieh* is a curious division of an animal face into two parts, each part one side and the two sides extended usually upon the curved surface of a vessel of some sort, joined together and remaining single in the middle at the snout and muzzle.[37] This figure,

[33] Creel, *Studies*, pp. 236-237; Creel, *The Birth of China* (New York, 1937), p. 116. Karlgren (*Bulletin of the Museum of Far Eastern Antiquities*, XXIII, 1951, 1) presumes to sneer at this, but offers no alternative explanation. I have not the least doubt that his disagreement is based on error.

[34] See Creel, "On the Origins of the Manufacture and Decoration of Bronze in the Shang Period," *Monumenta Serica*, I (1935), no. 1, plates; *Birth*, pl. VI; R. Wilhelm, *A Short History of Chinese Civilization*, tr. J. Joshua (London, 1929), p. 40, fig. 1; p. 41, fig. 2; C. P. Fitzgerald, *China: A Short Cultural History*, 3rd ed. (London and New York, 1950), pp. 108-121, figs. 9-21.

[35] Fitzgerald, p. 111, fig. 14.

[36] Fitzgerald, pp. 124-133, figs. 23-33; B. Laufer, *Jade: A Study in Chinese Archaeology and Religion* (Chicago, 1912), pp. 42-43, figs. 2-4; p. 162, fig. 74; pp. 258-260, figs. 162-165; pp. 316-317, figs. 198-200; pls. xxiv, xxxiii.

[37] Verbal descriptions in Creel, *Birth*, pp. 115-116; *Studies*, pp. 248-249.

sometimes merely a head with or without the lower jaw, has been the subject of endless controversy among sinologists.[38]

To explain it, I revert first to an opinion given almost half a century ago by Laufer, that it should be viewed "in the light of a deity."[39] I think it was a deity originally, long before the time when any of the examples of it we have, even the earliest, were made. I think that it was a relative of the earth deity of the Andean Society we have already got to know and of the similar, less important deity we are about to meet in the Middle American Society. This is as impressive as the close similarity which has been found between the conceptions of water and earth godhead in the Andean and Mesopotamian societies. The new, Chinese-Andean similarity is substantiated in a number of ways: by the techniques of representation by halving the face of the deity[40] and of rendering the figure with subordinate serpent themes and

[38] Creel thinks it sometimes represents one animal and sometimes another and that the term *t'ao-t'ieh* refers to the method of treatment and not to the animal represented; he is surprised that there is almost nothing in the later records to explain the figure; *Studies*, pp. 241-243, 251, n. 20; *Birth*, p. 117. Karlgren says (*Bulletin of the Museum of Far Eastern Antiquities*, II [1930], 41) that the figure is "nothing but a dragon mask. The dragon (*yang*, male) is . . . a regular fecundity-fertility symbol." This opinion comes near the mark, I think; certainly, the figure is a mask (see text below), but by "fecundity-fertility" Karlgren implies human as well as vegetal fecundity-fertility, and requires an important phallic element in that.

[39] P. 185.

[40] The halving of the face of the Andean deity has not been mentioned above, but it is to be seen clearly in figures cited in n. 15: Larco Hoyle, *Los Cupisniques* (Lima, 1941), figs. 212, 213, and 214. The halving in the Andean cases seems to be for the purpose of emphasizing the identity of priest-prince and deity, or the intimate representative function of the priest-prince, which could not be the purpose of the halving of the *t'ao-t'ieh* since the two halves are the same in the *t'ao-t'ieh*. But such entirely different application of the same kind of technical device is typical of what happens to culture traits diffused among different societies. There is a geographic link between the Andean and Chinese practices, which resembles the latter far more than the former, in certain practices of the northwest Pacific coast peoples of North America; see Creel, *Studies*, pp. 249-250.

themes of bird beaks and heads and other like procedures, and, most important, by the fact that the faces both of the *t'ao-t'ieh* and of the Andean cat-god were masks to be worn by priests representing the respective deities.

On the whole, I think it is probable that in the *t'ao-t'ieh* figure there survives the representation of a deity of the time of origin of the Chinese primary society, quite possibly of a deity who had been forgotten, or purposely obliterated, or so much changed in character as to be only vaguely recognizable in his new semblance. He may perhaps not have been a cat-god, but I have rather a strong impression from the many figures of him that he was.[41] More important, there is no proving that he was a chthonic god like Enki, Osiris, and the Andean cat-god. Serpents and dragons form his features and his body much more frequently than they do those of the Andean god, and, whatever this may have meant in the late second millennium and the first millennium B.C., it surely

[41] Rostovtzeff thought the figure was feline and related to the Persian horned lion-griffon (M. Rostovtzeff, *The Animal Style in South Russia and China*, Princeton, 1929, p. 70, cited in Creel, *Studies*, p. 240; *Birth*, p. 115), which is a possibility. A Han jade, figured by Laufer (p. 259, fig. 164), puts a part of a perfectly natural cat-face into a certain design where the *t'ao-t'ieh*, often a very much degenerated *t'ao-t'ieh*, appears: the lower jaw is omitted, as is often done, and the top of the head is replaced by conventional décor, but eyes, snout, whiskers, and fangs are startlingly realistic. This is most unexpected and intriguing. It seems to me that it must mean that the Chinese artist, even as late as Han times, had before him some instruction, or original drawing or other representation, which included a completely natural cat-face, and that he worked from that to produce the usually highly conventionalized, degenerated *t'ao-t'ieh* figure; in this particular case he began at the top and bottom in the usual conventional manner and then suddenly threw the instructions to the wind and carved the middle features of a perfectly natural cat-face. It might be supposed that this means nothing whatever for present purposes, but for one tell-tale detail, the pair of ferocious fangs standing out as they almost always do in the Andean cat-faces and as they do not, so far as I know, in the conventional *t'ao-t'ieh* figure. Whiskers, appearing on a number of the earlier *t'ao-t'ieh* figures, also suggest the feline origin of the figure. I cannot agree with Creel that the figure represents different animals in different cases (see n. 38 above); I think the differences arise simply from different ways in which the artists have applied their conventions.

must originally have meant that the god was very much a water god. I think we may take it that China had in its very early days a water-god as the other three societies had, but that we must leave it open whether he was a truly chthonic water-god.

Finally, we must entertain the idea that the water-god not only gave rain, well-water, and spring-water, but also river-water; this, for the reason that North China was progressively losing its rain at the time of origin of the civilized society. Myths going back to the first cycle, however, show plainly that the inundations of the Yellow River appealed to the popular imagination as something dangerous, something which necessitated diking and dredging of the river; Yü, greatest of the mythical heroes and possibly an original charismatic leader of the society, earned his reputation chiefly by digging a channel to contain the river flood. This need not mean that the Chinese were at no time grateful for the waters of the rivers. But there is no trace at all of anything like that extraordinary reverence the Egyptians developed for the annual flood of their single river, on which they wholly depended, so that their great earth-water-vegetation deity, Osiris, *was* the flood and arrived annually *in* the flood to sustain mankind. The Yellow River was not, of course, a single river for the Chinese as the Nile was for the Egyptians. The Yellow River had tributaries within the territory of the society. In fact, the society probably started on the tributaries as much as, or more than, on the main river. This may possibly explain the fact that the only surviving record of hope for a good river flood we have is for small rivers. "China's sorrow," as the Yellow River's flood is still called, may never have seemed to be the work of a beneficent deity.

The beneficence of water and its connection with deity are abundantly witnessed in India, but nearly all the evidence is late, a good deal of it consisting of modern survivals. A certain amount of the evidence is concerned with the general climate of India, in which the breaking of the summer monsoon and the dryness before it are prominent,[42] and to some extent this annual renewal of drought and relief from drought must have strengthened Indian feelings about water. But there are plenty of signs that the annual crisis in the weather is not the whole basis of the Indian devotion to water.

One of the most general manifestations of the sacred quality of water in India is the practice of representing deity in various ceremonies by a jar of water (*gatha*), which thus becomes the seat (*pitha*) of the god for the occasion.[43] How old this is, it would be hard to say, but, like other practices concerned with water, it is not of Aryan origin, for fire rather than water was the sacred expression of deity to the Indo-Europeans[44] so that there is some possibility that it goes back to the first cycle of Indian history. Another general manifestation is the ubiquity of sacred ponds, tanks, and baths and of the practice of ceremonial bathing in them. It is generally agreed[45] that this practice does go back to the first cycle, for there is at Mohenjo-daro a most elaborate

[42] The attack of Indra and the Maruts on Vritra, the "Demon of Drought," and the Danavas seems to be chiefly of this character. The same is perhaps true of the legend of Agastya, but, since this is probably of South Indian origin, it may have special sources there, notably sources concerned with great summer heat; see H. Zimmer, *Myths and Symbols in Indian Art and Civilization*, ed. J. Campbell, Bollingen Ser., No. VI (Washington, 1946), pp. 112-114.

[43] Zimmer, *Myths and Symbols*, p. 34; B. K. Sarkar and H. K. Rakshit, *The Folk-Element in Hindu Culture: A Contribution to Socio-Religious Studies in Hindu Folk-Institutions* (London, 1917), pp. 49 n. 1, 51-52, 73 sqq., 91, 96. Sometimes today it is not clear what deity the *gatha* represents—which only goes to show how important the water is!

[44] Zimmer, *The Art of Indian Asia*, ed. J. Campbell, Bollingen Ser., No. XXXIX, 1 (New York, 1955), p. 37.

[45] Zimmer, *Art of Indian Asia*, 1, 21; Sir M. Wheeler, *The Cambridge History of India*; Supplementary Vol., *The Indus Civilization* (Cambridge, 1953), pp. 29-31; E.J.H. Mackay, *Further Excavations at Mohenjo-daro*, 1 (Delhi, 1938), p. 20.

ceremonial bathing structure, including a public bath and also what may have been private baths for priests.

All rivers are to some extent sacred in India, and it is quite possible that this also goes back to a very early time. If Childe is right in identifying the Sarasvati with the Great Mihran,[46] then it probably does, for the mysterious Sarasvati is still one of the three most sacred of sacred rivers. The Indus is not now among them, however; the other two today are the Ganges and the Jumna, which, no doubt, recalls the establishment of the society in the Ganges basin in the second cycle. Sarasvati as a goddess was one of the wives of Brahma, the Supreme Deity, whose eminence as a god or as a theological-philosophical concept of being, may also be very old. In fact it is possible that the sacred character of rivers goes back to origins. If it does so in any form at all like its modern Indian form, it would be the only case of the kind among the primary civilized societies, so far as the evidence shows—which, perhaps, is a reason for supposing that it had another form at origins if it does go back so far.

The creator-deity of the third cycle of Indian history, Vishnu, together with his consort, Lakshmi or Padma, are just as closely and intimately identified with water as Brahma and Sarasvati: they *are* water, and every cyclic creation is made *in* water and *from* water. Lakshmi is indeed clearly of non-Aryan origin and can be traced back to the first cycle via southern India,[47] which reproduced many features of the early culture after they had been changed in the north. As creator, Vishnu is associated with Shesha, world-serpent and king of all serpents, who is a part of a part of Vishnu and is water as Vishnu is water. All serpents, of course, signify and symbolize water. They are in general beneficent. In fact, there have arisen among them *naga* kings and queens, guard-

[46] See Ch. I, n. 2.
[47] Zimmer, *Art of Indian Asia*, I, 158-160.

ians of mankind who direct the terrestrial waters. In southern India most ruling dynasties have claimed descent from *naga* and *nagini*. The descent of the serpent daimon or deity is itself shown to go back to the first cycle by figures on a seal found at Mohenjo-daro.[48]

And, in India the waters were in part waters of and in the earth, as they were wholly in Mesopotamia and Egypt.[49] They moved subtly as the serpent in the earth and made it fertile. But India had also another beast symbolic of water, the elephant. Elephants seem chiefly to have been concerned with the waters of the sky, for they were "cousins of the clouds [with] power to attract the rain clouds and to provide, thus, the enlivening element of water for the maintenance of the crops and, through them, of man and beast."[50]

The water-worship of the Middle American Society is something well known, and it certainly goes back to the origin of the society.[51] It was a very special kind of water-worship, as special as that of the Egyptian Society and quite different, for it was rain-worship, as has been noticed in the last chapter. And, as shown there, rain-worship of this pronounced and peculiar kind was the natural consequence of the rise of the society in a tropical rain-forest. As far as I know, there are very few occurrences of water other than rain-water in religion in the Middle American Society and those few that there are always represent other water as connected with rain.

In every part of the Middle American Society, in those extensions of the society outside the rain-forest just as much

[48] See pp. 156-157 below.
[49] Zimmer, *Myths and Symbols*, pp. 74-75.
[50] Zimmer, *Art of Indian Asia*, I, 160.
[51] The first evidence of it is in temple sculpture, and that does not go back to origins, but the ubiquity and great predominance of Middle American water-worship make it certain that it goes at least as far back as the origin of the civilized society.

as in those within it, the water gods were rain-gods, the Chacs in the Maya region, Tlaloc and the Tlaloque in the Mexican, the Cocijos in Oaxaca, and the Tajins in Central Vera Cruz. Often these deities were represented as giants. They had gourds in which they kept the water they poured upon the earth, and they were attended by frogs. Various misfortunes, happening in the myth, resulted in too much water being poured out—a contretemps easy to understand in a tropical forest. The rain-deities were often represented with traits borrowed from other water-connected symbols, including the fangs of the cat-god, and, especially in Mexico, serpentine traits.

All the rain deities were fourfold, one for each direction of the compass, as happened with many gods in Middle American religion. Together with the corn-god, the rain-deities held first place in popular devotion. So true is this that the society might be described as primarily a rain-worshipping society. The corn-god was probably more beloved than any other god. He *was*, in fact, the corn, and the farmer constantly and always felt his presence; he was there, allied with man, feeding man and supporting the entire human cause and life.[52] But the corn-god was not the power that the rain-gods were. Man had constantly to please the rain-gods, for they could withhold supplies when supplies were needed and they could, and constantly did, give their supplies in excess and in violence, causing floods, fungus, rot, and destruction.

The intimate association of the rain with the corn is reminiscent of the association of the inundation with the grain in Egypt, and, obviously, the same logic dictated this in the two cases. It is instructive to find the association emphasized in the two cases in which water came to the society in an especially forceful and dramatic way. The rain in Middle Amer-

[52] J. Eric S. Thompson, *The Rise and Fall of Maya Civilization* (Norman, 1954), pp. 234-240.

ica was also associated with the earth, as in most of the other societies we have studied. The earth cult in Middle America was a popular cult, and the earth was represented by a cat-god, a jaguar, as it was in Peru, but it appears that the relative importance of the earth-god and the rain-god was reversed in the two societies: in the Andean Society the earth produced water, or bore water on its surface, and so the dominating deity was the cat-god of the earth; in the Middle American Society the water came with dramatic force from the sky, not from the earth, but it fell upon the earth and caused it to produce grain and all other vegetal needs of man. Hence the rain-gods dominated the process of food production, and the earth-god held the secondary place.[53]

The association of the rain-gods with the corn-god and the earth-god were only two among an enormous number of associations which show clearly how important the pervasive rain-gods were.[54] Many of these associations were probably comparatively late developments effected by the priests as they enlarged the theology in order to hold the popular imagination. We need not here pay attention to that, but there are two associations which relate only to the Mexican part of the society (as far as we know), and deserve special consideration. They are with the goddess of lakes and rivers, Chalchihuitlicue (Lady of the Turquoise Skirt), and, in his character as the east wind (Ehecatl), with the great and famous hero, Quetzalcoatl. Both of these were certainly early. Chalchihuitlicue was the lady companion of Tlaloc, the

[53] I suspect this is why the full development of the ritual and symbolism of the cat-god was not accomplished until a relatively late date, the Classic period, as Americanists call it; see P. Armillas, "Tecnología, formaciones socio-ecónomicas y religiónen en Mesoamerica," *The Civilizations of Ancient America: Selected Papers of the XXIXth Congress of Americanists*, ed. Sol Tax (Chicago, 1951), p. 22.

[54] How pervasive they were is suggested incidentally in a study of Thompson's, "Aquatic Symbols Common to Various Centers of the Classic Period in Meso-America," *The Civilizations of Ancient America*, pp. 31-36.

chief of the four Tlaloque. Quetzalcoatl's original character may have been his character as culture-hero, but he became identified with the east wind which brought to Mexico its beneficent rain supply from the Gulf, and consequently his relation with the Tlaloque became a close one.

It is the special physiography and climate of the Valley of Mexico, so different from that of the rain forest, which explains the goddess also. The Mexican part of the society was grouped about the lake system of the valley, having from the lakes and rivers (in so far as they were not contaminated by nitrous infusion) a form of water supply which was of no importance elsewhere in the society's territory; hence Chalchihuitlicue. I should suppose that she survived from primitive times in the lake region, and that, when the rain cult penetrated from the lowlands with the expansion of the civilization, the priests—missionaries?—took her into the religion and allied Tlaloc to her.

The Cretan Society yields less significant evidence of the importance of water in early religion than the other six societies do. It is not that water had no place in the religion; certainly it had a place; but it is not possible on the evidence to estimate how important its place was.

If we see the religion of Crete, with Persson, as a unified and much elaborated fertility cult, then water had its place in the rites celebrating the advent of spring.[55] If we prefer to follow Nilsson and remain agnostic as far as possible, presuming to know only a series of isolated particulars, then spring-water, well-water, and rain all had their places.[56]

[55] Axel W. Persson, *The Religion of Greece in Prehistoric Times*, Sather Classical Lectures, no. xvii (Berkeley and Los Angeles, 1942), pp. 51, 89.

[56] Martin P. Nilsson, *The Minoan-Mycenaean Religion and its Survival in Greek Religion*, Skrifter Utgivna av. Kungl. Humanistiska Vetenskapssamfundet i Lund, no. ix, 2nd ed. rev. (Lund, 1950).

Other authorities, concerned chiefly with particulars that can be seen in the numerous ring-seals, the friezes, the figurines, and the cult places archaeology has uncovered, also tell from time to time of water in religious symbolism. Thus, Evans finds a pictographic rendering of summer drought and thinks there were rain-making ceremonies to counteract it,[57] and Dussaud discerns a tree cult in which rain played a part.[58]

The climate and physiography of Crete are such that there must always have been a water problem—and of that, of course, a fertility cult would in a general way be good evidence. The climate is a typical Mediterranean climate with a short rainy season, and the rain supply was certainly getting less when the settlers arrived and for long afterwards. Also, the island is so small that there are no rivers large enough or long enough to hold a sufficiency of water throughout the summer; in fact, there are very few which do not go dry. And there are no lakes—but these matters and the very special character of the intermount plains of Crete have been reviewed in the last chapter. It is hardly conceivable in these circumstances that the need of water conservation should not have found its way into Cretan religion.

As a matter of fact, there are plenty of indications that it did. Springs were sacred places. Most Cretan religious celebrations were conducted in the open air, many on the sides or tops of mountains; this latter could very well have happened because the celebrations had to do with the waters which flowed down the mountain sides in the rainy season and fertilized the plains. If we choose to think that that was so, then what became a highly developed fertility cult in the later days of the society may have started—and may indeed have

[57] Sir Arthur J. Evans, *The Palace of Minos, IV*, Part II (London, 1935), pp. 446, 450-452.

[58] R. Dussaud, *Les civilisations préhelléniques dans le bassin de la Mer Égée* (Paris, 1914), pp. 411-413.

continued—with a special emphasis on the water supply, but one which just did not leave a clear archaeological record. It may be that when at last the Cretan script is read there will be evidence to prove this. Already, the variety of different sorts of water ceremony proposed by different scholars is suggestive. But I am afraid we just do not have quite enough really telling data to draw a firm conclusion.

That certain water and earth symbols were common to three or four civilized societies at their origin and that the common symbols appeared on both sides of the Pacific are phenomena which demand explanation.

We do not know why the symbols mean what they mean, but only that they do so. The largeness and the slate-grey color of elephants (which are a water symbol in the Indian Society only) may be thought to resemble the same qualities in the appearance of rain-clouds; the suggestion is quite plausible, but there is no evidence to back it. Serpents are long and sinuous, like rivers; they also sometimes have holes in the earth through which it may be said that they move subtly, like water—but rabbits and other beasts have holes in the earth also. As for feline animals, there seems no reasonable similarity between them and earth which should explain their representation of earth in the manner of serpents' representation of water.

Clearly, no explanation of the widespread incidence of the serpent and cat symbols can be found in reasonable resemblances. These symbols evidently came to be adopted at some time in a limited region, or regions, and were thereafter diffused to other regions. When traits common to the two sides of the Pacific are found, it is usual to attribute them originally to the "circumpolar" peoples, and it has long been known that the early Chinese show affinities with those peoples.[59] That, then, might be taken to explain the common use of the serpent symbol by the Chinese, Middle American, and Andean societies and of the feline symbol too if, as has been supposed here, that symbol also was in use in China.

But how did the serpent symbol reach India? It is improbable that it was simply diffused there from the circumpolar region; there are rather a large number of mountain barriers in the way, and what little we know of early Indian peoples does not suggest that they had anything much else in common with circumpolar peoples. I think the explanation of this difficulty is that the circumpolar peoples were not the ultimate source of this symbol, or perhaps of the cat symbol though that is far harder to trace. The serpent symbol is probably of Near Eastern origin. It is found both in Mesopotamia and Egypt, but not in the prominent place it came to hold from India eastward.[60] But this is no surprise: it is a well known phenomenon of diffusion that traits retain their original character in peripheral regions, not in the central region in which they originate. This seems to be what happened to the serpent symbol.

But when did this migration of the symbol occur? Evidently at an early date, for the relatively humble roles of the serpent symbol in Mesopotamia and Egypt were already established early in the time of the civilized societies there, if

[59] Creel, *Studies*, pp. 246-247; Ralph Linton, *The Tree of Culture* (New York, 1955), pp. 524-525; C. W. Bishop, "The Beginnings of Civilization in Eastern Asia," *Annual Report of the Smithsonian Institution, 1940* (Washington, 1941), p. 443.

[60] In Egypt the serpent became the god Apophis, enemy of the sun and ruler of the darkness of night, the darkness probably a reminiscence of the serpent's chthonic character. The connection with water seems to have been entirely lost (although I shall not be surprised if some Egyptologist can find a survival of it). In Mesopotamia the serpent was still chthonic, but it had come to represent the power of survival and of generation, the former at least having a completely logical connection with water in the vital function of water which was at its maximum importance at the time of origin of the civilized society. Cf. the place of the serpent in the Gilgamesh myth, for which see *The Intellectual Adventure*, pp. 208-212.

indeed they did not antedate the civilized societies. I suppose, therefore, that the serpent symbol in its earlier, more important meaning was carried in all directions by the great mesolithic dispersion from the Near East of the Old World.[61] It would in all likelihood have had to be as early as that to reach the New World early enough for the origin of the Middle American Society. In fact, I rather suspect that cultural kinship through the circumpolar peoples usually means sharing in the mesolithic dispersion and diffusion from the Near East rather than a relationship in which peoples living about the North Pole played a central, originative part. It would not surprise me if the cat symbol came from the same origin even though there is no trace of it there in any earthy association.

It is, presumably, not necessary to warn the extreme diffusionists of the limited significance of the migration of the symbols. The migration of symbols does not connote as well the migration of a whole culture. It does not necessarily denote the migration even of the practice or thing signified by the symbol although usually, and certainly in the present cases, much of the practice had also migrated. Thus, serpent and cat symbols in several different civilized societies cannot be taken to mean that the whole culture of each of those societies, or any considerable part of it, was originally one and was diffused as one huge complex from one place to all the others. It cannot even be taken in any large sense to show an original connection between the religions of the several primitive societies. In the present cases it shows only that the particular belief and practice which each symbol denoted migrated, it does not exclude a good deal of modification in beliefs and practices in each separate occurrence of them, and

[61] Creel (see n. 59) finds a number of other traits which the Chinese shared with the circumpolar peoples, some extending to other peoples and some not. He notices (*Studies*, p. 249) more distant resemblances with "Scythian" products. See also Rostovtzeff in n. 41 above.

it shows nothing whatever about their places in the religion of each society—of this last ample evidence has already been given. The formation of the religion of each society was a separate series of events. There was, of course, similarity of circumstances and causes in the formation of all the religions, and that is in part why similar beliefs and practices arose in them all—similar beliefs and practices which, together with the symbols denoting them, had existed among the various peoples at an earlier time when they were all directly or indirectly in contact with one another. It may be said that the similarity of circumstances and causes served to select the similar beliefs and practices from the common inheritance and to emphasize and develop them.

The limited significance of the migration of symbols in no wise lessens the significance of the repetition at the origin of all the primary civilized societies of essentially the same main facts. The repetition in case after case of the concern of the religion with the need for water is enormously impressive. The gaps in knowledge and the tenuousness of some of the evidence are not enough to invalidate the obvious implication of the positive evidence. The best provisional conclusion we can draw from it is that the concern of religion with water was general to all the societies and that there were mere differences in expression of the concern from one society to another, most of them the consequence of environmental differences. If new evidence should appear and should throw doubt on this, it will be time then to modify or abandon the thesis. The probability is at present that all the primary civilized societies were in search of a reliable water supply at their origin, that the need for water and the securing of it were such serious matters that they became a prime concern of the societies' religions, and that the finding and securing of a reliable water supply was a causal factor in the origin of the primary civilized societies.

Such a probability is not at all surprising since all the peoples involved in these great events had been plagued with the problem of water supply literally for millennia. They had, no doubt, had respite from it at some periods, but they were certainly not enjoying a period of respite on the eve of the foundation of the civilized societies. The primitive farmer on the margins of a desert, where the water supply usually tended to decrease, was threatened with shortage even apart from increase of population induced by his need for extra hands at seed time and harvest. Nor may we assume that the danger of shortage was coeval only with cultivation. It had been one of the pressures which led to the discovery and development of practices of cultivation, for the mesolithics had suffered from it too—which is neatly confirmed for us by the sharing of symbols for water and earth. Consequently, we must think that fears for the water supply were already firmly embedded in the minds of the founders—if that is a realistic term—of the primary civilized societies before the foundation took place. What happened when it did, then, was a specialization out of feelings already deeply ingrained and certainly already expressed in religious terms.

But specialization is too weak a term to express fully the sort of change in religion which occurred when the first civilized societies took form and substance. In Chapter 1 I have argued that *new* religions with charismatic leaders then arose. The new religions were formed on the basis of old feelings deeply ingrained, which, however, were raised to new and indeed desperate fervor. If anybody doubts this, he will find it solidly proved by the concrete new results in ecclesiastical-political organization which followed upon the propagation of the new religions and the establishment of the civilized societies; but these matters are not treated in this book. There remains one more matter to be dealt with in this chapter, a survey of elements other than water worship in religion at the origin of the primary civilized societies, so far as it proves possible to discover them.

It is significant that the other elements in religion are far harder to get at for the scholar than water cult is. Thus, for Egypt, a round dozen deities, only about half of them of importance, appear in the Memphite Theology. The First Dynasty, to whose establishment the document relates, does not, of course, occur early in Egyptian history; it occurs only at a point early in our effective knowledge of it. But it is possible to see in the document that some of the gods were already old—as has been done above in the case of Osiris. Thus, Atum must have been old then, so that we may guess that sun-worship was established at an early time. There is some reason for supposing, however, that sun-worship arose in the Delta and that the Delta was drawn into the civilized life of Egypt at a time after the origin of the society.[62] Horus and Seth were probably old too, but whether they were respectively sky-god and earth-god, or were simply two local deities from different parts of Upper Egypt whose priests

[62] It is pretty sure that sun-worship originated in the Delta, and probably at Heliopolis, where it is known from the Third Dynasty onward, but the Egyptians did not consider the east, the direction of the sun's rising, the primary direction of outlook until a comparatively late date (I think they actually came to do this in the course of re-creating their religion during the decline of the society at the end of its first cycle); earlier than that the south was most important to them, and that is usually thought to be because the high culture first arose in the south, the main valley of the Nile, where the most important fact of nature was the river, which came to Egypt from farther south; see John A. Wilson, in *The Intellectual Adventure*, p. 43; Baumgartel, *The Cultures of Prehistoric Egypt*, pp. 19-24 and *passim*. But the latter work should be used with caution; I take no stock in Mrs. Baumgartel's view that the Delta region was brought very late into the civilized society; cf. above, Ch. 3, n. 17.

had been notorious rivals, or whether they were neither of these things, it is not possible to say.[63]

For Mesopotamia, Anu, Enlil, and Ninhursaga were all in early historical times regarded as senior in some sense to Enki. Ninhursaga was indeed earth, and, as such, was intimately involved with the fresh water which Enki embodied. But Ninhursaga was not simply earth, chiefly or only important because of its relation with water, as was the case with the cat-god in the New World societies. Ninhursaga may have been that originally, and, if she was, she should be added to the cat-gods to strengthen the similarity between Mesopotamia and the New World societies in the matter of water worship. But she was also a mother, *the* mother, prototype of the goddess of human fecundity as that becomes well known to us in the later civilized societies of the Near and Middle East. And she may already have existed with this character at the origin of the Mesopotamian Society.

As to Anu and Enlil, both represented elemental natural forces, and it would, I think, be over-skeptical to refuse to accept those forces as their respective original characters. Anu was a sky-god, as Horus perhaps was, but in the record we have of Anu he is so distant, so aloof and impalpable, that we know almost nothing about him. He was, however, the presidential deity in the earliest organized pantheon we know of in Mesopotamia. And Enlil may well be described as his chief executive officer. During the part of the first cycle of

---

[63] At least, I think it may be said that they were of similar origin and almost surely that they originated, or were first established in Egypt, in the same general region; for the difficulties which arise from thinking them of different origin, see Kees, *Der Götterglaube*, pp. 256, 258-259. Frankfort (*Kingship*, pp. 21-22, 183) thinks the two represent the principle of struggle between opposites in the cosmos; cf. W. B. Kristensen, *Het Leven uit den Dood* (Haarlem, 1926), pp. 19-20. I very much doubt that such a sophisticated idea could have been understood at the origin of a primary civilized society, but it may have come to be held in a later, more scholarly age.

Mesopotamian history which we know from literary sources, the latter part, Enlil was to all intents and purposes the chief deity. He acquired a special character as god of the state, patron of the political arts.

Frankfort thinks that Enlil's pre-eminence was due to the pre-eminence of the theologians of Nippur, Enlil's home city.[64] It is likely, I think, that political ambitions went with the theological pre-eminence, even though they may have been relatively mild and peaceful political ambitions. Nippur was not one of the oldest cities of the society—and very probably Enlil was no older than Nippur. Moreover, the exaltation of a deity by a feat of theology cannot have been accomplished very early in the society's history. Excellence in theology—or philosophy; it does not matter which word is used—is a mark of culmination of a society's intellectual development, and that does not happen at the society's origin.

As a matter of fact, the conception of a fourfold leadership among the gods, the leadership of Anu, Enlil, Ninhursaga, and Enki, shouts to heaven of the work of theological schools, inspired by ecclesiastical-political motives. Anu, it would seem, was an earlier leading deity, probably the immediately foregoing leading deity. To make him president, or to admit his presidency, would serve as a sop given by the new political authority to its predecessor whose sanctity it was unwise to flout. And Enlil's political skill is very suggestive, as are his theoretical deference to Anu and his position as Enki's elder brother. A skillful priesthood, claiming hegemony over the society for itself, or for an *isshaku* (city prince, tenant of the city god), could well have acknowledged Anu's presidency, while emptying it of substance, and have claimed close kinship for their god, Enlil, with the earliest great god, Enki, while asserting superiority to the latter by seeing Enlil as the

[64] *Kingship*, pp. 216-217.

elder and Enki as the younger of two brothers.[65] Ninhursaga probably did not figure largely in the transaction, for, in all likelihood, she had always been closely associated with Enki.[66] But now, to insure the junior position of that still beloved old god, he was ranked below his own spouse. Is it going too far to see in that a special innuendo?

I do not think, then, that Anu or Enlil shared place as important gods with Enki at the origin of the Mesopotamian Society, still less that they excelled him. Ninhursaga may already then have been closely related to Enki though we do not know that she was, but, if she was, that simply enlarges somewhat the scope of the original water-earth worship. This does not mean at all that there was monotheism at the origin of the Mesopotamian Society. Other deities, possibly quite numerous ones, spirits, daimons, tutelary gods, especially the last in Mesopotamia, all of them inheritances of the primitive past like Enki himself, may have been revered, and even Anu and Enlil may have been among them. But I think none of them was Enki's equal; Enki was the god of the hour.

For India, the archaeological remains of the first cycle, on which we again rely, show three main elements besides the probability of water worship. The first is a female deity, a *gramadevata* much like the household deities of the type

[65] The suggestion that this is what Enlil's champions did does not imply on my part a "belief in the unlimited envy and competition of ancient priesthoods," which so outrages Frankfort (*Kingship*, p. 349, n. 6). They probably did it in the sincere conviction that they were serving the best ends of deity and of humanity. Such a frame of mind is a far firmer basis for bold and ambitious action than envy and competitiveness, and priests, by the whole nature of their training and tradition, are most given to it.

[66] Jacobsen in *The Intellectual Adventure*, pp. 137, 157-158, 161-164. In the latter of the myths here (pp. 161-164) recounted by Jacobsen, it is shown that Enki had once had a function later claimed for Enlil, the making of mankind. In both myths (pp. 157-158 and 161-164) it is likely that Enki is being discredited by Enlil's champions, for in both Enki was doing things which the Mesopotamians did not approve of and perhaps hated.

today, an earth mother concerned with fertility. The second is the phallic worship—the *linga* and *yoni* both represented—again surviving today. And the third is the representation of a god looking much like Siva, wearing horns, sitting like a yogi and surrounded by beasts, Siva in his character of Pasupati in fact. It seems sure that the female deity was an inheritance from pre-civilized times, and it is very possible that the same is true of phallic worship and even of Siva since he was probably then, as now, connected with phallic worship. One representation of Siva, on a seal, shows attendant serpents at the sides, as well as human worshippers, and so may be thought to have been connected with water worship.[67] But we have no indication in this evidence of how important these other cults may have been in comparison with water worship at the actual time of origin of the society.

The Indian cult looks as a whole like a fertility cult, water playing a specially important part in it, and the same is true of the Cretan cult, as we have already seen. For Crete indeed there is no basis for thinking that there were at origins any but the female deity, or deities, about whom the fertility cult centered. The problematic male deity was probably a late innovation. If there were other aspects than fertility in early Cretan religion, we are wholly in ignorance of them.

We are much in the dark too as to early Chinese religion. There is a probability of an important astronomical-seasonal element in it, but there is not the least warrant for considering this as an original element. As a matter of fact, we know of such a development in every other primary civilized society except the Indian Society, and there is a possibility of one in the Indian Society as well.[68]

[67] For an illustration, see Zimmer, *Art of Indian Asia*, ii, pl. 16.

[68] But it must be admitted that this is unsure; some "rayed" figures thought to represent the sun, may not represent it in an astronomical, but purely in a theological, sense. See Ernest Mackay, *Early Indus Civilizations*, 2nd ed., rev. D. Mackay (London, 1948), pp. 68-69.

Another, and far weightier, consideration for China is the age of the ancestor-cult. Since such cults are well known among primitives, it is quite possible that the Chinese cult may go right back through the time of origin of the society. But, since new religious practices often enter civilized societies at a transition from one cycle to another, it is also possible that ancestor-worship came to China in late Shang and early Chou times when (in my opinion) such a transition was occurring.[69]

Evidence for religion in the Andean Society goes back to an early date. Supported by the evidence for the Mochica period, several centuries later, it might be thought to show that earth-water worship was the original religion of the society, which only later expanded in other directions. But I am afraid that the evidence is too slender to be made to bear so definite a meaning. There is a general probability that South American primitives worshipped ancestors, and that they had other devotions as well, and there are distinct suggestions for later times in the history of the civilized society that ancestor worship occurred there.[70] Hence the

[69] It was exceedingly popular during the main part of the second cycle, during most of the Chou period, that is to say, but weakened after that. The evidence of the oracle bones carries it back, so far as the Shang royal family is concerned (Creel, *Birth*, p. 178), which makes it probable for all the upper classes, into the fourteenth century B.C. I think it is safe to say that for a thousand years from that time it was the dominant religion of the society. There are examples in history of strong prevalence, hardly quite dominance, of the elements in religion over two successive cycles in the history of the same civilized society, but they are not common. On the whole, therefore, I think it likely that ancestor worship came to China in the second cycle, that is to say, in late Shang and early Chou times. This agrees with the opinion of C. W. Bishop; see "The Beginnings of North and South in China," *Pacific Affairs*, VII (1934), 302.

[70] Bennett thinks that evidence of it exists for the Mochica period on the northern part of the Andean coast and for the Nazca period (probably not much later) on the southern part (Wendell C. Bennett and Junius B. Bird, *Andean Culture History*, American Museum of Natural History Handbook Series, no. 15, New York, 1949, pp. 177, 179-180). The trouble with the evidence about the Andean Society, for present as for other pur-

case of the Andean Society, at least on its own merits, must be left open.

Middle America we know better, and it is quite possible that ancestor-worship occurred there at the origin of the society.[71] A fertility cult is a probability also. It is hard to find evidence of any original important gods except the rain-gods and the maize god. The maize god was indeed an important deity, a close ally of man, but he depended upon the rain gods. Another deity of some importance was, possibly, Huehueteotl, as he was called in later times, the fire god, whose later name (we know no earlier one) means "the old god." But he may not really have been very old,[72] and certainly he was local in his origin to a part of the society which was not, in my judgment, the part where the civilization originated. He belonged to the region of the volcanoes.[73] There is also Quetzalcoatl in his capacity as a culture hero. He was possibly a leader of migrants from Vera Cruz or Chiapas to the Valley of Mexico, or he brought certain prac-

---

poses, is that it is too local and scattered; we need good archaeological sequences for many more regions of the society than we have at present. I think what we do have is enough to show that the cat-god became and remained a general object of reverence even if there were revolts against it in some times and places; such revolts are common enough in history. But I do not think the evidence is at all sufficient to show what other developments, especially what later developments, were important, widespread, or sustained.

[71] If it is not customary to describe Middle American practices of honoring the dead as ancestor-worship, they were certainly akin to it; cf. the ceremony described by Eric Thompson and his references there to other ceremonies (*Rise and Fall*, pp. 217-223).

[72] Vaillant suggests that the corn deity may have been older; G. C. Vaillant, *The Aztecs of Mexico*, Pelican Book (London, 1950), p. 58.

[73] I have followed Armillas' outline (in *The Civilizations of Ancient America*, pp. 22-23) of the religious practices of the Formative stage, and I can indeed find no indication elsewhere, except in the case of Quetzalcoatl, of other possible deities. I have taken the funerary mounds he discusses suggestively to be signs of ancestor worship. That they became more numerous later would be natural enough as the society developed, and the same may well be true of the Andean Society, though for that we lack sufficient evidence.

166

tices to Mexico from that general region. He too, then, how-ever early in Mexico, belonged to a part of the society other than its region of origin, and cannot be included among the earliest deities.

I shall make a bold summing up of this scanty material, for I think it contains certain probabilities even though it is scanty. A few gods of the more obvious natural phenomena seem to be the possibilities at the origin of the primary civilized societies. Thus Egypt and Mesopotamia offer a possibility of a sky deity, and China does too although I make no suggestion as to the name by which the Chinese one was called. The sun does not seem to figure much, nor the moon. The earth may quite possibly have been revered in a larger way than simply as the producer, with water, of vegetation. The earth may have been considered as a sort of mother to mankind in the Near Eastern societies and India, although I doubt very much that analogies between earth's functions as mother of man and of plants, or as a source of fecundity in both, belong to such early times. Ideas of that kind sound more like the invention of later, learnedly poetic priests.

Fecundity of man may have been part of religion, but there is not much authority for it; the best authority is really its greater likelihood before the rise of the civilized societies among primitive farmers who wanted help on their farms and perhaps the strength of numbers for protection against enemies, human and animal. But Ninhursaga, as she is known later in Mesopotamian history, stood for fecundity, and it is usually assumed, without evidence, that the Cretan goddess did so. There is some actual evidence for a fecundity cult in the Middle American Society, and the Indian *gramadevatas* were certainly goddesses of fecundity. Karlgren sees evidence for a fecundity cult in China also,[74] but there is no compulsion

[74] "Some Fecundity Symbols," *Bulletin of the Museum of Far Eastern*

to believe him, either as to its existence, or as to its being the original form of the ancestor cult and of other elements in Chinese religion.

Ancestor worship is suggested in the evidence for the Middle American Society, and it may have existed in the Chinese and Andean societies as well, weak as the evidence is in those cases. But I doubt that it was limited to those three societies, numerous as the similarities between them are. Rather, I suggest that all the primary civilized societies had some way of honoring dead ancestors, again because practices of the kind are so common among primitives. Just what forms this honor took in the different societies, it is impossible to say, but I think the question is whether these earliest civilized peoples simply remembered their ancestors with respect and affection, or whether they thought their ancestors had power over them for good or evil. Probably in all cases they thought their ancestors survived in some way and so took some measures to make the new life pleasant for them. At what point the latter belief became a belief in the power of dead ancestors is difficult to decide, and I do not think we have any more evidence to show that that dividing line had been crossed in China at origins than we have for any other of the primary civilized societies.[75]

Besides sky and earth gods, fecundity cults, and ancestor worship, there were certainly plenty of animistic beliefs, zooduly, beliefs in tutelary or familiar spirits, and possibly other inheritances from primitive times. The real problem is how strong any of these inheritances were in the crucial periods when the primary civilized societies came into existence. Inasmuch as it has proved difficult to discover any-

---

Antiquities, II (1930). For an opinion about Karlgren's doctrine, see Creel, *Studies*, and cf. n. 38 above.

[75] See n. 69 above.

thing about them, it might be deduced that they were not strong enough to leave a great impression, the impression of "great gods," but that some of them *were* strong enough to leave relics enough for intelligent and speculative-minded priests to get hold of later and in some cases to turn into something new and influential. Also, clearly, they left a lesser impression than the deities of water worship who have been investigated, for, difficult as it was to find out anything about the water deities, it proves still more difficult to find out anything about the other elements in religion.

From such differential lack of evidence we may deduce that water worship, or water and earth worship, was the really effective belief at the origin of the primary civilized societies. Other elements in religion were not obliterated. Perhaps they too caught some of the novel enthusiasm, but they cannot have fully shared place with water worship, for they had not the special answer to the question of the hour. What seems to have happened is that water worship was selected from among the general religious fund of the proto-civilized peoples and magnified to serve in overcoming the crisis which threatened the peoples' survival.

We have the choice, in the almost complete absence of evidence, of thinking that new religion began to be formed after settlement in the new habitat, on migration to it, or before departure from the old habitat. My guess is that it began before departure from the old habitat, that it began in response to the rise of the danger which drove the peoples to migrate. But the positive elements of novelty must surely have been added at and after re-settlement, when water in abundance had been found, when hope had been added to fear, when, perhaps, the god was making manifest his munificence.

There is evidence for some of the societies, notably the Andean and Mesopotamian societies, of the new religion first emerging in quite a small, limited area of the society and thereafter spreading outwards. The novelty so spread must be taken, I think, to have been a coherent formulation of a complete gospel, including the new and the old, the positive aims developed in the new habitat and the terms of escape from danger in the old. In the Mesopotamian case it looks as if the first settlers formulated the gospel and then passed it on to later ones, or that the later ones imitated it. But there must have been other societies in which the new gospel arose in one corner and then spread elsewhere to other, already established settlers, and yet other societies in which there arose competing revelations, eventually to be amalgamated or to supersede one another. Such variations of process are probably of minor importance. It is of more importance that all settlers, whether or not they, or their leaders, were formulating coherent religious doctrine, were in the state of emotion to receive and to believe a plausible doctrine which expressed their recent experience in a convincing way and gave them satisfactory assurance of their issue out of danger and into attainable, though no doubt conditional, security.

We discern, then, the coming together of peoples to form a society, peoples in a certain, definable state of emotion, and the subsequent spread among them of a religion. It was Émile Durkheim's opinion, derived from shrewd insight, but from insight applied to a kind of situation very different from the rise of the primary civilized societies, that the assembling and "concentration" of peoples was necessary to produce a "mental exaltation" in which new social life could be awakened.[76] In the cases we have here under observation the

---

[76] *Les Formes élémentaires de la vie religieuse: Le Système totémique en Australie* (Paris, 1912), p. 603. The whole passage is worth considering for the partial parallel with the origin of the primary civilized societies:
"Pour que la société puisse prendre conscience de soi et entretenir, au degré d'intensité nécessaire, le sentiment qu'elle a d'elle-même, il faut qu'elle s'assemble et se concentre. Or, cette concentration détermine une exaltation de la vie mentale qui se traduit par un ensemble de conceptions idéales où vient se peindre la vie nouvelle qui s'est ainsi éveillée; elles

170

"mental exaltation" was given by the circumstances anterior to the assembling of the peoples. But the assembling and concentration may well have been factors in those cases also; I think they were. In the final chapter of this book that matter will be considered a little further, and will be related to the ultimate essentials of the material circumstances of the primary civilized societies.

---

correspondent à cet afflux de forces psychiques qui se surajoutent alors à celles dont nous disposons pour les taches quotidiennes de l'existence. Une société ne peut se créer ni se recréer sans, du même coup, créer de l'idéal."

I suggest that (whether or not Durkheim's view of the case before him was correct) the chief difference in the cases of the primary civilized societies is that, besides formation of self-consciousness, there was a powerful interjection from immediate catastrophic external forces, forces which we may conceive under the idea of nature, but the settlers, no doubt, conceived differently.

CONCLUSION: THE MEANING OF

THE ADVENT OF

CIVILIZED SOCIETIES

THE meaning for man, and perhaps for more than man, of the advent of civilized societies may be expressed in three propositions. The first has to do with the distinct and separate origin and individuality of each civilized society; it gives certain consequences of the individuality of civilized societies—a rationale of their individuality. The second seeks to explain the process of origin of the primary civilized societies and in particular the effective elements of environment and of the acts and beliefs of men in the process. The third is an attempt to show what the novelty of civilized societies is and how such a novelty came to emerge. The three propositions are formulated out of what has been discovered in this book. They do not constitute a final characterization of civilized societies, for some of the material on which they are based is not final and sure. But they serve as a summary working statement of what happened when civilized societies first arose, and they offer an initial insight into the possible significance of the career of civilized man in as much of its course as that career has covered since it began six millennia or more ago.

It has been shown in Chapters 3 and 4 of this book that the seven primary civilized societies were each of separate and distinct origin. The falsity of the various theories of their common origin, or derivation one from another, argued in Chapter 1, has thus been proved. That the societies were of separate origin is essential to an understanding of the causes and process of their origin. Their separate origin is important further in that it shows that major events in the career of mankind can and do happen repetitively—even to seven instances. History, with nature behind it, repeats itself.

But it must not be forgotten that the major repetition of causes and process was accompanied by incidental differences, some of them impressive. Five societies arose in river valleys, one in a small island and another in a tropical rain forest. The significance of the more important of these differences will be shown in the statement of the second proposition, for the differences as well as the major repetition are necessary to reach understanding of the causes and process of origin of the societies.

There soon arose important likenesses between the societies which were not merely the consequence of the repetitive character of the societies' origin. The societies borrowed many culture traits from one another. How particular traits were acquired, whether by borrowing or invention, is, however, a vastly unimportant matter by comparison with how a society itself originated, for a society is in no wise at all the sum of its culture traits. Only persons most miserably deluded by archaeology's sticks and stones could fall into error about that.

Every trait, indeed—every institution, every practice, every artifact and thing—in each society was marked with the individual aesthetic style of the society, however much like

173

corresponding traits of other societies in form or function it might be. This was shown in Chapter 1 on the authority of Kroeber.

The style of human societies is worked up most dramatically in their fine arts—the finer, the more dramatic, the more powerful in effect. If this is elementary, it must be kept in mind in considering elemental things at the origin of civilized societies. In this study the fine arts have been considered in particular in Chapter 5, where the sharing of certain symbols in religion between the Indian, Chinese, Middle American, and Andean societies was studied. Symbols, depicted by artists, were used for the purpose of religion just as much in the other three societies as in the four which happened to share some symbols. The use of the arts for religious purposes is, in fact, one of their most important uses, not only in the primary civilized societies, but in all societies, civilized and primitive.

Religion was the positive, the human-mental, agency of the creation of the primary civilized societies, and it has been so in the creation, or re-creation, of all civilized societies. One of its specific functions has always been to unify a society and give it a common purpose. It is reasonable to think, therefore, that the aesthetic style of a society may serve to that end. The style gives, immediately, a sharp and powerful recognition of the individuality of the society to its members. The recognition is a dynamic, inspiring experience for them. It works upon their emotions and imbues them with the feelings, the purposes of the society, and particularly of its leaders, require them to experience. It would seem, then, that the specialty of a society's style is no mere accident, but a vital factor in the society's being.

This completes the first proposition.

The need of water for survival was the crucial need of those peoples who brought the primary civilized societies into existence; this was a recrudescence of a need many peoples had experienced before, and it had occasioned a long series of notable innovations in the material (and, no doubt, nonmaterial) culture of primitive societies. When the primary civilized societies arose, they did so not only with specially large and reliable sources of water, but also, in six cases out of seven, with an inexhaustible soil. Primitive man may have stumbled upon such soils here and there at earlier times, but, if he did, no evidence survives of any particular consequences of his doing so.

It is proposed now that the quality of the soil in the six societies, the Egyptian, Mesopotamian, Indian, Chinese, Cretan, and Andean societies, facilitated the close concentration of the peoples of the societies in relatively small areas on a permanent basis, and afforded them a great new opportunity to increase their numbers. Other physical factors may have contributed to the concentration and the increase, the limited area watered and inundated by the rivers in five cases out of six and in the sixth, the Cretan case, the smallness of the island. In the Indian, Chinese, and Andean cases ready accessibility of adjacent inhabitable land, not having the same water or soil supply, may have drawn off some population, but it is quite evident that this did not materially alter the growth of population in the main sites.

Are the growth and concentration of population and the physical basis in soil and water to be accounted, then, as causal factors in the origin of the primary civilized societies? If they are, what about the odd case of the Middle American Society which had no inexhaustible soil even though it did have a voluminous and dependable water supply?

The Middle American Society is also remarkable in that its original nucleus, the forest territory at the base of the Yucatan Peninsula inhabited by the Mayas, had no cities in the full sense of the term. It had only great ceremonial centers where the people gathered temporarily on the frequent occasions of religious celebrations.[1] At other times they were scattered through the forests, living not at all concentrated as the peoples of the other primary civilized societies were able to do. As has been observed in Chapter 4, the Middle American Society was also remarkable for its very wide extent as a whole. Although it was quite certainly a single society since the unity of its religion is fully manifest, it had, in fact, three or four main territories, probably all separate from one another, from an early date—not actually from origins—and it may have had a number of smaller separate regions also. In this respect it was quite unlike all the other primary civilized societies. It would appear that the wide extent of the whole society and the scattering of its people at least in its original nuclear territory are two aspects of the same peculiarity, namely that the society could not, as the other six primary societies did, concentrate itself in a very small total area where the soil was fantastically productive and was either renewed every year, or, as in the older, loess area of the Chinese Society, was inexhaustible to the untiringly industrious farmer.

The reader, no doubt, discerns the direction in which this argument is leading, but he must be warned that it is a speculative argument; the proposition the argument is building up cannot be taken as proved. The warning given, however, we proceed.

It goes without saying that all the other primary civilized societies also had important and frequent religious celebrations. The proposition requires, therefore, that those celebrations were independent of, and anterior to, the physical basis which facilitated the formation of the society. This does

---

[1] See J. Eric S. Thompson, *The Rise and Fall of Maya Civilization* (Norman, Okla., 1954), p. 44 and pp. 57 ff.

not mean that none of the physical basis was necessary; it is hard to conceive that the water supply was not necessary. But it does mean that the special soil, a part of the physical basis in six cases out of seven, was not necessary. No reasonable doubt can exist that, where such a soil was available, there the origin of a civilized society was strongly promoted, but, water and perhaps other advantages of which we do not know being available, a special soil was apparently not essential. It would be very interesting to know if the character of the land in Middle America offered any direct or indirect substitute for a special soil, but, if it did, I am ignorant of the fact. To be sure, abundant rain, available at all times when it was required, is an easier water supply to manage than great rivers with their inundations, but it is not possible to say whether this was a sufficient compensation for the poverty and inaccessibility of cultivable soil.

The effect of this proposition is to show how extremely important in the formation of a civilized society its religion was. We know this very well already so that the proposition gains somewhat in plausibility. Religion could serve to give the settlers in great river valleys the courage to clear the land, to keep it cleared, and to bring the water to it. It could also, if the proposition is true, serve to encourage settlers in a rain forest to undertake the far greater task of clearing the land in a tropical rain forest, where, however, the water came direct by the grace of the water deities.

The Middle American case suggests something not immediately obvious from the evidence of the other six societies—it suggests how important the actual assemblies for religious celebration were. If this appears to be elementary and obvious, it is another of those elementary things which are also elemental. Its meaning is to be found in that "mental exaltation" produced in peoples assembled and concentrated for religious purposes which was cited at the end of Chapter 5 from Émile Durkheim's profound interpretation of religious experience in societies of a kind very different from the primary civilized societies.

We may not leave this matter without enquiry into the importance of water cult as such. Its vital importance on the occasions before us is now abundantly clear, but we should know also whether it must be considered a permanently inherent feature of all civilized religion. Obviously, it must not. There is a survival of it in most religions of civilized societies, no doubt, in anxiety about food and gratitude to deities which are supposed to give food. These feelings certainly descend to some extent, becoming generalized and weakened in the process, from devotion in the primary civilized societies to the gods or goddesses who gave water—and were in several known cases gods or goddesses of agriculture or, more broadly, of fertility. An exception is the Indian Society in which water is still sacred, and this could—at a hazard—be ascribed to the annual course of the weather in India, where the monsoon breaks suddenly after long drought. Even so, the Indian water cult of today looks, not so much like the water cults we know at the origin of some of the primary civilized societies, as like a series of abstractions from an earlier, more explicit cult made by priests to keep alive in people's minds the devotion to water.

The upshot is, then, that water worship is not a permanent and inherent feature of religion in civilized societies. Its great importance was temporary, though probably not shortlived, at its maximum at those seven crucial episodes with which this book is concerned, the origin of the seven primary civilized societies.

This completes the second proposition.

In our preliminary enquiry in Chapter 1 it proved difficult to find fundamental differences between civilized and primi-

178

tive societies. The cyclic rise and fall process was found to be peculiar to civilized societies, but otherwise little could be found which is not reducible to mere quantitative terms. Both quantitative differences and cyclic rise and fall will have their place in the statement of this third and final proposition, which is also the final explanation to be offered in this book of what happened when the primary civilized societies emerged. We approach that explanation by seeking to narrow down the differences between primitive and civilized societies functionally (for which purpose a little outside evidence will be called in). Is there anything which primitive peoples cannot do and civilized peoples can? If so, is the reason simply quantitative, or is there any other factor involved?

It is impossible to hold, today, that there are insurmountable intellectual barriers which set limits to the competence of primitives. All notions of that sort were exploded with the overthrow of Lévy-Brühl's theory of primitive mentality.[2] There are certainly problems to be encountered in teaching primitives the complexities of modern Western technical devices, but no greater problems than in teaching the same things to the simpler members of the Western Society itself. And, since other civilized societies have not produced similar technical complexities, even those problems could not arise in diffusion of functions between them and primitive societies. Nobody, presumably, will suppose that there could be any barrier between civilized and primitive societies in the arts. It takes time and experience for the people of one society— whether civilized or primitive—to learn the feeling and to follow the technique, where it is highly developed, of an art of another society—whether primitive or civilized—but this can always be done. Nor will anybody think that the arts of primitive societies are inferior to those of civilized societies,

[2] By E. E. Evans-Pritchard in "Lévy-Brühl's Theory of Primitive Mentality," University of Egypt, *Bulletin of the Faculty of Arts*, II, Part I (1934), 1-36.

at least anybody in the modern Western Society, whose paint-
ers, sculptors, and musicians, running short of native themes,
have turned largely to primitive sources for themes to borrow.
We have seen in Chapter I that, although writing was
almost certainly invented in civilized societies, the process of
invention was one of developing and adding to practices
which primitive societies shared with civilized societies. It
is now to be observed—and it is really in no wise surprising—that there are no insuperable obstacles to teaching
primitive peoples to read and write, or to reducing their
languages to written form and teaching them to use them
so. Yet that is a somewhat misleading remark, for the ini-
tiative in such undertakings need not come from a civilized
source. Primitives can undertake this for themselves, once
they have seen the device in operation in civilized societies.
It is only necessary to mention Sequoya, author of the Chero-
kee syllabary, to establish the competence of primitives for
this very special task.[3]

As to higher thought—philosophy, the broader and deeper
conceptions of science, and a number of related intellectual
adventures—the comparison is less simple. In all that is
purely speculative, depending on creative exercise of imagination, primitives are quite the equals of the civilized. Consider,
for example, what may be called the "metapsychology" of
the peoples of the Upper Niger region in the interior of West
Africa,[4] or the spirit world of the Nuer of the southeastern
Sudan.[5] It is very possible, probable indeed, that these African

[3] For other examples, see, e.g., David Diringer, *The Alphabet* (New
York, 1948), pp. 151-157, 178-181. There must have been many other cases
of which we have no record.
[4] See G. Dieterlen, *Les Âmes des Dogons*, Université de Paris, Travaux
et Mémoires de l'Institut d'Ethnologie, no. xl (Paris, 1941), pp. 73-91,
126-140, 246-247; *Essai sur la religion Bambara* (Paris, 1951), pp. 56-65.
I am indebted to my colleague, Professor Robert G. Armstrong, for bringing the African evidence to my attention.
[5] See Evans-Pritchard, *Nuer Religion* (Oxford, 1956), pp. 28-105.

peoples have attained their speculative heights with the aid of diffusion to them of the subtleties of Memphis, Thebes, and Alexandria, not to mention later and more distant sources. But that is not the least indication that they could not have achieved the equivalent for themselves; indeed it is very possible too that some of the diffusion went in the reverse direction.[6]

But there is a great difference in the levels of critical thought attained in the two sorts of societies. Indeed, it may be suggested that speculation, as known to us in primitive societies, is wider and freer than it is in civilized societies just because in primitive societies it remains relatively little checked by criticism. The direct explanation of the difference is, I suggest, simply the larger knowledge of the physical world that a civilized society acquires from its vastly greater and (usually) more varied environment; studying such a greater body of knowledge comparatively, scholars are sure to correct the unbridled speculation of an earlier age, a good deal of which, in fact, is inherited from primitive sources. And here we have to observe something else too: time is of the essence of critical thought; civilized societies begin their careers with cosmological, theological, and other large hypotheses no different from those of primitive societies. The myths considered in Chapters 3, 4, and 5 show this. It is not until the age of reason that criticism gets seriously to work, eliminating contradictions and inconsistencies, systematizing,

[6] Cf. Frankfort, *Kingship and the Gods: A Study of Ancient Near Eastern Religion as the Integration of Society and Nature* (Chicago, 1948), p. 363, n. 20, where the metapsychology of the Shilluk is instanced. This is simpler than that of the Dogon and the Bambara of the Upper Niger (see n. 4); it is like that of the Nuer (see *Nuer Religion*, p. 144), who are neighbors of the Shilluk. These varying African concepts may be the origin of Egyptian concepts, or vice versa; we cannot tell. *Kingship*, pp. 61-69, makes very interesting comparative reading with the two passages from Dieterlen's works cited in n. 4. For this whole question, see also Paul Radin, *Primitive Man as Philosopher* (New York, 1927).

and scaling down some, but by no means all, inheritances from an uncritical past.[7] Once this process begins, however, it moves fast, for the high rate of change characteristic of civilized life operates in thought just as in other functions. This is yet another quantitative distinction between civilized and primitive societies.

Yet even severe critical standards can be learned by primitive societies—although those which have learned them have usually done so as a part of the process of absorption into a civilized society. It is, in fact, clear that primitives can learn all that civilized peoples have to teach. Much of what the latter do have to teach is of a secondary character. Probably nearly all of it is either simplification or elaboration: short cuts and quick devices—these especially in thought[8]—or else developments of method by complication for limited purposes. It is hard to discern anything in this which is not ultimately quantitative.

On the other hand, it is historical fact that primitive peoples did not invent these ideas and practices and civilized peoples did. Is it possible to imagine hypothetical circumstances in which primitive peoples might have invented these things for themselves? The answer, I believe, is very simple: they might, indeed would, have done so if the development of human societies from the time of the emergence of agriculture had

[7] Frankfort had a fair appreciation of the difference between critical thought, as in the age of reason of civilized societies, and the speculative thought of primitive societies and of the age of faith in civilized societies; he identified the latter with mythopoeic thought. See *Kingship*, p. 362, n. 4; Frankfort, Frankfort, Wilson, Jacobsen and Irwin, *The Intellectual Adventure of Ancient Man: An Essay on Speculative Thought in the Ancient Near East* (Chicago, 1946), *passim*. In the latter of these two works all the authors make some contribution to the thesis about mythopoeic thought. Although this is a great contribution to the subject, I think the Frankforts have made gross errors in where and when they find mythopoeic thought.

[8] Most fall within the category Toynbee calls "etherialization" (A. J. Toynbee, *A Study of History*, III, London, 1934, pp. 174-192). The term is, I think, inappropriate, but the formation of a category useful.

continued at a gradual, evolutionary tempo. Sooner or later in an evolutionary course the circumstances requiring those devices and specialities must by the laws of chance have arisen. This affords us our last important insight into the manner of origin of civilized societies: it was a revolution, in fact a series of seven revolutions, each one having essentially, and indeed very closely, the same course and results as the others.

We have found when the revolutions occurred: they occurred when primitives left their remaining refuges in the desert belts and sought new refuges in river valleys or other formidable places where there was plenty of water. We have found why revolutions occurred: they occurred because the old refuges no longer had sufficient material resources to support their inhabitants and the inhabitants' survival was gravely threatened. Like all changes properly called revolutions, these seven revolutions occurred with great rapidity. They occurred between the time when the peoples caught up in them left their previous homes and the time when they began the formation of the civilized societies in the new sites to which they migrated. We cannot fix either of those times precisely, and we have reason to think that in most, or all, of the seven cases the civilized society did not emerge until after the peoples had spent some time—some generations, or even centuries—at the edge of the sites, or in other regions marginal to them, probably learning how to live in the sites. But nobody will doubt that the time needed for these experiments was a very short time as compared with the duration of primitive societies, or even with the duration of the civilized societies themselves.

The consequences of the revolutions, seen at first glance externally, were as great as the time they took was small: the consequences in each case were the conglomeration together of hundreds, probably thousands, of primitive societies to form one society, which therefore, in an additive manner of speaking, was hundreds or thousands of times as great as the primitive societies of which it was formed. But the conglomeration was more than mere addition; it was a form of that concentration in the religious life of a society, twice recently cited above, to which Émile Durkheim attached so much importance. Only in that state of exaltation could men have made the revolutions through which the primary civilized societies were formed. Yet how much was accomplished in that state of exaltation? Was conglomeration fully equivalent to consolidation?

Henri Bergson has put forward a doctrine which has bearing upon this question. He conceives of a distinction between static religion, which exists to bind a society together and hold it solid against outsiders, and dynamic religion, which opens a society to all mankind and seeks to bring all mankind into one society.[9] It is a valid description of what happened positively in the revolutions with which we have to deal. We have discovered how, in all probability and in all cases, water worship became a great new gospel enlarging and supplanting the old static religion very much in the manner Bergson lays down,[10] and how in each embryonic civilized society all the constituent primitive societies came to accept the same new gospel. We have seen too in some of our seven cases something which did not happen to attract Bergson's notice, the plastic arts brought into service of the new religion to represent it in symbols and the creation of a special idiosyncratic style by each society, expressing its aspirations and ideals.

But Bergson does not show how far the consolidation went. He simply says that civilized societies became, as

[9] *Les deux sources de la morale et de la religion,* Swiss ed. (Geneva, n.d.). For the closed society, cf. W. G. Sumner, *Folkways* (Boston, 1940), pp. 12-15.
[10] Bergson, pp. 201 ff.

184

primitive societies had been, closed societies,[11] which might be thought to require that full consolidation occurred. It is certainly true that religious exaltation died down gradually after the revolutions were accomplished—so far as they were accomplished—and that religion became static again. Water worship, we have found, was of temporary importance, however vital it was at its crucial time. Civilized man went on to other things. He was led on, in fact, to bring his new physical environment more and more under his control, to make it adjust itself to him rather than to adapt himself to his environment. This in reality has been his sustained and most characteristic achievement, and his success in it still daily inspires and allures him.

But his civilized societies, as societies, show a record of quite remarkable instability. Their consolidation has certainly never been complete. Their arts indeed have been vigorous, at least for limited periods, maintaining and developing, each in its way, the distinctive style of its society. If it were not for these successes and for the conspicuous manifestation of styles and feeling both in the arts and in all their activities, civilized societies could scarcely be considered to be societies at all. But the arts only announce aspiration. Accomplishment comes afterwards if it comes at all.[12] Even externally, in political form, civilized societies have reached unity only in the late centuries of each cycle of their existence, and in the earlier stages of the cycle have been conspicuous for disunity and, at times, for internecine military struggles of appalling magnitude.

And at the end of every cycle in its history every civilized society has fallen into decline and there have emerged, or tended to emerge, from it small units quite analogous to the

[11] p. 31.
[12] See Benedetto Croce, *Aesthetic as Science of Expression and General Linguistic*, trans. D. Ainslie (London, 1929), pp. 50 ff.

primitive societies which were originally conglomerated together to form the seven primary civilized societies.[13] The logic of this is clear enough, now that it is known how the primary civilized societies were formed. At the collapse of a civilized society indeed Bergson's doctrine and Durkheim's doctrine as well have come to apply again, for a new religion has arisen and a new revolution has occurred. The cyclic revival has begun, in fact, and the society has been re-created, or a new society created, by conglomeration of the remains of the old society and of new territory and peoples also.

But the history of those cyclically repetitive episodes is the history of civilized societies as they have developed after origin and until today. This book may end, therefore, with two questions about that history. Did the advent of civilized societies usher in an era in human fortunes which is merely transitional, an era in which there has been no securely established society but merely a series of attempts to form societies? And, if so, will the attempts ultimately be successful or unsuccessful?

[13] Cf. *Feudalism in History*, ed. Rushton Coulborn (Princeton, 1956), pp. 190-192 and *passim*.

INDEX

Abu Shahrain, *see* Eridu
Abyssinia, 42, 43, 76
adaptation, adjustment, to environment, 21, *32-33*, 185
Aegilops, 41n
Afghanistan, 40, 41, 88
Africa, African land, territory, 37, 42n, 43, 56, 58, 59, 180
Agastya, 148n
age of faith, 20, 114, 142n, 182n
age of fulfilment, 20
age of reason, 20, 181, 182n
agriculturalists, agricultural peoples, societies, 33, 75, 95, 117, 120
agriculture and agricultural regions, *39-66*; Abyssinian, *42-43*, 65; Chinese, *50-54*, 57, 65; eastern Old World, *43-50*, 53, 54, 57, 65; expansion of, derivation of, 42, 45n, 64, 65-66; grain, 9-10, 11, 12, 32, *40-43*, 47, 49, 53, 54, 55, 60, 61-62, 65; Middle American, 55, *61-62*, 63, 64, 65; mounds of earth used in, 62, 65-66; New World, *54-65*, 119; North China, 42n, 49, *50-54*; origin of, 39-40, 44n, 45-47, 49-50, *54-66*, 94n, 159; planting, 47, 62; plant breeding, 47, 49n; sowing, 47, 50; vegetables other than grains, 10, 40-41, 44n, 45, 46, 47, 55, 61, 100-101; Venezuelan-Colombian, 55, 56, 59, 61, 62; western Old World, *39-43*, 42, 43, 45, 46, *47-50*, 53, 54, 57, 62, 65, 69, 76, 78; western South America, *62-64*, 65, 103. *See also* amaranths, barley, kaoling, maize, millet, rice, wheat
Akbar, 25n
Alaska, 55
Alexandria, 181
Allbaugh, L. G., 121n, 122n, 124n
alpaca, 64
al Ubaid, 81, 83, 131
amaranths, 60, 61
America: Central, 64; "Indians" of,

15; Middle, 126; North, 15, 50; South, 57n, 59. *See also* New World
Ames, Oakes, 49n, 50n
Amratians, 76, 77, 78
Amri, 88n
Amur River, 70
Anatolia, 41n, 120; Eastern, 40, 92
ancestor cult worship, 164, 165, 166, *168*
Andean coast, coastal plain, 58, 59, 106, 109; desert, 5, 63, 99, 100
Andean Society, 4, 5, 9, 11, 12, 17, 18, 29n, 67, 108, 134, 145, 156, 174, 175; art forms of, 136-138; extension beyond original site, 175; origin of, *98-104*, 106, 107, 127; religion of, miscellaneous elements in, *165-166*, 168; religion of, water in, *135-140*, 152, 165, 169
Anderson, Edgar, 41n, 45n
Andersson, J. G., 34n, 53n, 96
Andes Mountains, 5, 63, 64, 98, 99; eastern slopes of, 103; western, 103
Anhwei, 92
animal worship, *see* zooduly
animals, domesticated, domestication of, 10, 39, 47, 48, 49, 62, 76. *See also*, alpaca, cattle, dogs, goats, llama, pigs, sheep, turkeys
animism, animistic beliefs, *see* beliefs, animistic
Antevs, Ernst, 33n, 34n, 59, 59n, 118, 119n
Anu, 161-163; as presidential deity, 161; as sky-god, 161
Apophis, 156n
Arabian coast lands, 43, 43n
Arabian Desert, 33, 35n
Arabs, 16
aridity, *see* desiccation
Armenoid peoples, type, 38
Armillas, P., 152n, 166n
Armstrong, Robert G., 180n

187

of primary civilized societies, 103-104, 112, 114, 118, 121-123, 124

myth, myths, mythology, 14, 72, 91n, 93, 94, 96, 97, 111, 133n, 156n; Andean, *100*; Chinese, 89-91, 100, 105, 141, 147; creation, *72*, *73*, *79-80*, *83-85*, 85n, *89-91*, 99-100, 114, 123-124; Cretan, *123-124*; conglomerate, 72n, 94n, 113, 114, 123; Egyptian, *73*, 83, 85n, 89, 133n; flood, 89-91, 93, 99-100; Greek, 123-124; Indian, 83-85, 85n; Mesopotamian, *79-80*, 83, 89, 100; Middle American, 151. *See also* Atum, Ch'e-you, *Enuma Elish*, Gilgamesh, Kung-kung, Niu-kua, Nūn, Yü

mythopoeic thought, *see* thought, mythopoeic

naga, 149, 150
nagini, 150
Nakada I, *see* Amratians
Nakada II, *see* Gerzeans
nation, nations, 20n
Natufian peoples, 46n
Nazca period (Andean Society), 165
Nazca River, 101n
Near East, 3n, 4n, 19, 31, 32n, 36, 37, 45n, 46, 73, 97, 124, 156; as center of invention of mesolithic practices, 27, 28, 29, 30, 37, 39, 45n, 50, 157; as source of migration of mesolithic peoples, 27, 28, 29, 37-38

necessity in social development, 128, *176-178*

Neolithic, Lower, Middle, Upper (Crete), *see* culture
Netherlands, 44n
New World, 38, 39, 49, 54-66, 68, 157

Nile River, 3, 11, 12, 70, 73, 75, 106, 126n, 147, 160n; Delta, 132n; Delta, Rosetta branch of, 74, 75; singularity of, 140; wadies of, 139

Nilsson, Martin P., 153

Ninhursaga, 161-163, 167; as earth, 161; as mother, 161; in relation to water, 161; as spouse of Enki, 163

Nippur, 162
Niu-kua, 90, 91
non-literate societies, 9
North China Plain, 97
North Equatorial Current, 56, 58
Nubia, 43, 76
Nuer, 180, 181n
Nūn, 73

Oaxaca, 111, 112, 151
obstacles to settlement in river valleys, *see* settlement in sites of civilized societies, physical task of
Oceanus, 124
Ordos, 105
Osiris, *130-134*, 138, 160; as creator, 130; as inundation, 131; as king, god-king, 132; as original god of Egyptian Society, 132-133; immanence in grain, 130, 147; immanence in water, 130-131, 147; in earth, 130, 146, 147; in Memphite Theology, 131; at Abydos, 132; at Memphis, 132; origin of, 132-133

Pa, 91, 93
Pachacamac, 101n
Pacific Ocean, 55-56, 98; islands in, *see* islands in Pacific
Padma, *see* Lakshmi
palaeolithic, palaeolithics, *see* culture, palaeolithic
Palestine, 40, 46n
parallels, historical, *see* similarity of development, dissimilarity of development
Pasupati, 164
Peloponnese, 4, 110
Pendlebury, J.D.S., 18n, 120n, 121n, 122n, 123n, 124n, 125n, 126n
Percival, J., 41n, 42n
Perrot, G., 124n
Perry, W. J., 27

196

The Library of Congress has cataloged this book as follows:

Coulborn, Rushton. The origin of civilized societies. Princeton, N.J., Princeton University Press, 1959.

200 p. 23 cm. i. Civilization, Ancient. i. Title: Civilized societies.
CB301.C73 (901.9) 59-5594 ‡. Library of Congress